THE BACKPACKER

BY ALBERT SAIJO

DRAWINGS BY GOMPERS SAIJO

101 PRODUCTIONS
SAN FRANCISCO

WITHOUT WHOM

For helping me get it together, thanks to: Jay, Judy, Oma — Aaron — Fred, Mary Ellen and Kodak (bear) — Don and Pat — for a dry, warm room. Locke McCorkle for getting me there. Peter Xiques. Barnaby. Matthew and Livia. Gary Snyder, who said to me, "It can be like tea ceremony." Lee, Rani and Eric. Dan and Dale Bacon. Thurston. Elin. Lynne. And as always to Ann, Paget, Drew, Banda, Peter and Ipo.

OM   AH   HUM

Second Printing, Revised edition

Copyright © 1972, 1977
Albert Saijo and Gompers Saijo

Quotation from *Ishi in Two Worlds* by Theodora Kroeber (page 13) Copyright © 1961 by The Regents of the University of California; reprinted by permission of the University of California Press.

Printed and bound in the United States of America

Distributed to the book trade in the United States by Charles Scribner's Sons, New York

Published by 101 Productions
834 Mission Street
San Francisco, California 94103

Library of Congress number 77-1523
ISBN 0-89286-116-9

CONTENTS

INTRODUCTION

No one has worked out a backcountry style as light, simple and elegant as that of the Himalayan yogi. Milarepa, the 11th-century Tibetan saint, at one point in his life had his outfit down to a few religious objects and a bowl. He needed no more protection than a thin cotton cloth because he had mastered the yoga of vital heat that enabled him to stand extremes of cold. He needed no bedding because he never lay down, spending most of his time in the posture of meditation. He needed no special supply of food. He made a soup of nettles that grew along the way. He hardly ever came down from the mountains.

Milarepa was in the ancient tradition of the mountain men of the Eastern religions—rishis, arhats, yogis, the Taoist outdoorsmen of China. All were in wilderness with the purest intention, for the only right reason. Uplift. Some could subsist on air, which is even lighter than freeze-dried food.

There are also stories in the Bible of men who traveled very light. Jesus went into wilderness 40 days and ate nothing. John the Baptist traveled the wilderness of Judea in camel-hair raiment and leather girdle, eating locusts and wild honey.

When we think of these outdoor styles and the very spare outfit they were based on, we begin to understand the enormity of our concern with food and equipment.

Closer to home, the Indian of the North American continent is forever a model of minimum and ultralight in a wilderness setting. Then we have the example of John Muir in going light. He had a beautifully austere backcountry style that contrasted perfectly with his exuberant nature. He carried no equipment to speak of, the clothes on his back and an overcoat or blanket—sometimes not even these—a tin cup, sugar, tea and a bag of bread or raw oatmeal which he would make into patties and toast on a heated rock next to his fire.

But we are who we are, living in the times we do, and for better or worse, we have our way of doing things. We've evolved a backcountry style that requires a certain amount of equipment. We've been weaned on a diet that emphasizes variety. Yet we do at least think of lightness and simplicity as ideals, even if we don't go as light and simple as the Himalayan yogi and John Muir. We're no longer into the backcountry style of the pioneer—cutting his swath through wilderness—and this must be considered an improvement.

It's absolutely essential at this time to develop a backcountry style that leaves no trace. The pressure of numbers on wilderness has become such that there's no alternative. No more bough beds. No more cutting down saplings for building shelters. No more large fireplaces. No more digging pits in the ground—not even hip holes.

Practicing campcrafts in wilderness is no longer appropriate, and modern equipment makes it unnecessary. A stove eliminates the elaborate fireplace. The down sleeping bag with polyurethane pad does away with bough beds and hip holes. With the light tarp shelter or tent there's no need for sapling frame structures.

We shouldn't think, however, that backpacking has reached its final form with us, as regards either food or equipment. We may well work our way back to Milarepa. Ever simpler, ever lighter.

So it's a provident and saving backcountry style we want. Lean. Ultralight. Appreciative of the wild as a refuge and sanctuary where we go to shake off the dust of the world. And because we know wild earth to be a kind of flesh, we go in a way not to wound it. We go light. As though, being stalked, we don't leave a trace.

Without a doubt, there are ironies involved in using wilderness-saving equipment given to us by a wilderness-spoiling technology. But dwelling on them would hold us back, we wouldn't be able to move, and move and change we must. However, let's keep in mind the deeper implications of the wilderness style of the mountain yogi and John Muir, not only in terms of their approach to food and equipment, but also their whole conception of the wilderness life.

WHY BACKPACK?

Why backpack into wilderness? Why leave the conveniences of technology, the pleasures of urbanity? What could be more absurd than packing 30 pounds or so through rugged country for days at a time. Yet more and more people are doing just this. Why? Isn't it in answer to a call from far back inside us? Beneath our urbane sophistication, isn't there a strong memory of existing at basic survival levels in wilderness?

There are still members of our species who roam wilderness in nomadic bands. Even our continent was the realm of savage cultures till very recently. (Was even the Stone Age so very long ago?) Can we believe that the savage within ourselves—the one who belongs to the woods—is dead? That savage in us appears to be very much alive. It is our savage eye that sees behind the conveniences and pleasures of our world to the earth-spoiling that supports them. The savage wants out. He wants to be expressed.

Backpacking in wilderness can be a beautiful and highly satisfying way to express the savage in modern terms. It's a fine sport. A high form of play. A way of honoring our beginnings. It's a deep recollection of what we once were.

The backpacker wants wilderness. The outback. Backcountry. Anywhere that roads have not penetrated. The government has set aside natural, unspoiled areas of great scenic beauty as wilderness and primitive areas. In these areas, roads, buildings and other forms of permanent occupancy are prohibited. The only access is by trail. You can pack in with horse and burro or, in some instances, go in by canoe. But wilderness is pre-eminently the domain of the backpacker.

As the pressures of industrial civilization and the rational madnesses of cities increase, the more need there is for the wilderness experience. In the city, our insanities are mirrored in all the people and situations we meet. Wilderness, on the other hand, doesn't reflect insanity well. Stepping into wilderness and looking past ourselves, we see the vivid space of great forests, mountains, rivers and deserts. You might say the wilderness experience gives us a standard by which to measure our sanity.

Backpacking calls out the wilderness inside ourselves, and we're always surprised by its sane and gentle nature.

WHICH FOOT FIRST?

Having decided to backpack into wilderness—and each person comes to it in his own time—where do you start?

Unlike camping out of a car, camper or trailer where you simply tune your motor, pack along most everything you want and go, backpacking requires a finer logistic. There are more complicated preparations to be made. It is a more demanding exercise of the whole person. It is more austere and more solitary.

There is also this difference: Your physical condition is not so important in car-camping. If you can drive a car, you can car-camp, and then you don't generally walk far afoot. Backpacking is walking with weight on your back and that can be strenuous. Perhaps this matter of physical condition would be the best way into the subject of how to start preparing for a backpack trip.

WALKING

Living as we do in a civilization committed to mechanical mobility, we fall into patterns of riding rather than walking; we walk only when there isn't a ride. Backpacking is walking. Wilderness is where we walk to. The best way to get into shape for backpacking is to start walking whenever you don't have to ride.

Adjust the schedule of your life so there is time to walk. Even in the city, it's possible to take long and interesting walks. Try walking to and from work. Walk during your lunch hour. Don't use the elevator, walk up and down stairs. It's good for the wind—the heart-lung system should be as sound as possible, especially for backpacking in mountains. Bicycling is an excellent way to get into shape for backpacking, but it has one disadvantage—it does little to strengthen the feet. Tough feet are essential in rugged walking, and there is no way to toughen them except by walking.

In addition to walking more in the course of doing chores, find off-time for day-long hikes in country close by home, someplace where you can stride out into natural scenery. Is there a state or local park nearby—a protected watershed, perhaps, with trails through it? If there is, get to know it.

HOW TO WALK

Offhand, you might think that no one can teach you to walk differently than you do. But if you work at it you can change your style of walking to some extent—and for the better. You can develop a walk that will carry you hour after hour without undue fatigue.

• **The Step** First there is the matter of gait or step. It should be well coordinated and easy. The right gait for you will carry your body comfortably upright and let you breathe easily and deeply. A slightly toed-in step makes the most effective use of the foot and leg muscles. It also gives you a better sense of body balance than a toed-out gait.

In the book, *Ishi*, by Theodora Kroeber, there is a description of how Ishi walked. Called "the last wild Indian in North America," he is said to have been a tireless walker.

> He springs from the great toe which is wonderfully strong in its plantar flexion and abduction. His method of locomotion is that of rather short steps, each foot sliding along the ground as it touches. Neither the heel nor the ball of the foot seems to receive the jar of the step. The foot is placed in position cautiously, not slammed or jammed down. He progresses rather pigeon-toed, and approximates crossing the line of his progress each step.

This appears to be a description of barefoot walking. It shows a walking style matched to a life style. The Indian had to walk quietly and far. Ishi's flat-footed, pigeon-toed walk was matched to his short step. This step would seem to be the most comfortable to the bare foot.

The modern American step tends to be long, a step designed for a hurried pace. And wearing shoes makes it a heavy step. The long step tends to bring the heel down first. It is probably the rubber-heeled, tight-supporting shoe that allows us the long step; without such a shoe, it would be too jarring.

Since we are trained to the long step and shoes, our hiking step will have to accommodate them. Without a doubt, a flat-footed gait is easiest on our feet. It distributes the weight of our body and the weight of whatever we might be carrying evenly over the whole foot. It spreads the jar of the step over the whole foot. Now a flat-footed gait depends on toeing-in for it is toeing-in that flattens out the foot.

If, then, the flat-footed, toed-in step could be combined with the long step, we would have the ideal hiking step, or so it would seem. And there appears to be a way to do this. Putting a "roll" into our long step seems to turn in the toe and flatten out the foot. The ideal hiking gait would seem then to be one with a long, somewhat rolling motion that brings the foot down toed-in and flat. The foot should come down lightly and spring off the toes strongly. The leg should be relaxed at the knee, but not so relaxed as to make your walk bouncy. This step is in contrast to what might be called the "military" or "pendulum" step.

• **Stride** A consideration of stride, or length of step, is also important. The stride should be measured and even where possible. A steady, even stride is essential to well-paced walking.

• **Pace** Pace is your rate of movement and is determined by your capacity as a walker, the distance you want to cover, the time you want to do it in, and the nature of the terrain. You have paced yourself well if you arrive at your destination at about the time you figured, tired perhaps, but not exhausted. This may not be important on a day-hike which ends at your car, but in wilderness at the end of the day's hike you must still have energy left to set out your camp, do chores and cook supper. A good pace has rhythm.

• **Rhythm** Rhythm is the variation you play on pace and stride. By varying the length of your stride—without breaking it—and slowing or speeding up the pace, you give your walk rhythm. How pauses and rest stops are spaced is a part of rhythm, too. The rhythm you established over the length of a walk is what you think of most, consciously or unconsciously, when you think of whether the walk made it or not. Rhythm is what measures the success of a walk.

WALKING IS MORE THAN WALKING

Walking is more than just walking. It's a way of being aware. Once you've got your walking technique down you can forget it. Then you are a body walking through space-time. You are there and your legs are moving you. Work on such things as the gauging of distance and time while in motion. Be aware of direction. Be conscious of the passage and course of the sun as a means of orientation while you walk. Have some idea of the length of days and the shifting point at which the sun rises and sets through the year. Be alert to weather and how it changes. Attend to landmarks. Get into the habit of backsighting along the way you've come. Be attentive to feelings of thirst and hunger—try carrying the minimum of food and water so that you learn your capacity to withstand their lack while walking. Learn to get the feel of country you're walking through, so that you could recognize it by this means alone were you to pass through it again. The feel of country is your total response to it. Be conscious of yourself walking and of something constantly new opening out before you.

Most important, get to know your capacity as a walker. Have an honest assessment of your strength as a walker so that you don't take on more than you can handle. This is especially important in wilderness, whether you are alone or in a party. We are talking about walking and hiking—ambling and sauntering are other and delightful matters.

READING

Getting into shape for backpacking means your head working for you as well as your body. If you have an idea of where you want to go, there is probably some literature about it. There are excellent guidebooks now on a wide variety of wilderness areas. History books, if available, can add to the enjoyment of your trip. Books on natural history can give your trip yet another dimension. To be able to botanize is a pleasure. To know the animals you meet seems a friendly thing. To understand something of the geologic force that shaped the land you pass through is humbling, and nothing adjusts your sense of what is important more than the vastness of geologic time.

Read books on wilderness in general. A little or a lot of John Muir is a must. No man depicts so well the nature and fascinations of wilderness or the spirit with which we should go into her. Investigate the current politics of setting aside and preserving wilderness areas. Read at least one of the "how to survive in wilderness" books. See Recommended Reading in Appendix.

WHERE'S WILDERNESS?

A little reading of some government publications can be quite helpful in locating wilderness. Our national parks and forests offer vast backpacking areas, including reserves designated by the National Wilderness Preservation System.

The Bureau of Land Management (U.S. Department of the Interior) has under its jurisdiction 457 million acres of public-domain land, much of it open to backpackers. Some Indian reservations allow access to their lands.

The National Scenic Trail System is developing trail systems throughout the United States. Two great trails have been designated so far—both over 2,000 miles long—the Appalachian Trail and the Pacific Crest Trail. Within the system, there are plans to include the Long Trail through Vermont, the Continental Divide Trail, sections of the Lewis and Clark Trail, the Natchez Trace, parts of the Oregon Trail and segments of the Santa Fe Trail. There is also a plan to develop a Pacific Northwest Trail to run east-west from Glacier National Park to the Olympic Peninsula and the Pacific Ocean.

The recently initiated National Wild and Scenic Rivers System allows access to back-country along free-flowing, primitive and un-polluted rivers. Land access to these rivers is restricted to trails and backcountry roads. You might try canoeing in.

Some state parks furnish backpacking country, though most are too small and overcrowded. Good areas remain in Baxter State Park in Maine and the Adirondack Forest Preserve in New York.

More and more private timberlands have been opened to the public.

About 90 percent of Canada's land area remains undeveloped. These vast areas of wilderness include not only national and provincial parks, but also extensive "crown lands"—much like U.S. public-domain lands—under the jurisdiction of the provinces. Through a system of fire and travel permits, much of this wilderness is open to backpackers.

PUBLICATIONS

The following are some publications—mostly from the U.S. Government Printing Office—describing wilderness areas:

Search for Solitude (about the National Wilderness Preservation System), U.S. Government Printing Office, Washington, D.C. 20402.

National Forest Vacations, U.S.G.P.O.

Backpacking in the National Forests, U.S.G.P.O.

Backcountry Travel in the National Park System, U.S.G.P.O.

Camping in the National Parks, U.S.G.P.O.

Public Access to Public Domain Lands, U.S.G.P.O.

Our Public Lands (Bureau of Land Management quarterly), U.S.G.P.O.

Trails for America (about the National Scenic Trail System), U.S.G.P.O.

Plans for Studies of Wild and Scenic Rivers, Bureau of Outdoor Recreation, U.S. Department of the Interior, Washington, D.C. 20402.

Public Outdoor Recreation on Forest Industry Lands, American Forest Institute, 1835 K Street, N.W., Washington, D.C. 20006.

For information regarding Canadian national and provincial parks, write to Canadian Government Travel Bureau, 150 Kent Street, Ottawa,

Ontario. For information about Canadian crown lands write to Department of Forests and Parks at the capital of the province you're interested in.

CATALOGS

Retail mail-order stores specializing in backpacking equipment usually print an illustrated catalog of their goods. These are available on request and are generally free. Send off for a number of them and study them closely. There is no faster way to learn about equipment. If you combine your study of catalogs with a reading of G.A. Cunningham's *Lightweight Camping Equipment*, you will have an excellent comprehension of what constitutes quality in backpacking equipment, especially in sleeping bags, packs and clothes.

A good catalog is fascinating to read. When a new edition of a favorite catalog comes in the mail, you put everything else aside and read it from cover to cover. With its combination of illustrations and text it is a distinctly modern form of literature. It is some kind of exercise in definition. See the list of outdoor stores on pages 186-187.

MAP READING

There is still another kind of reading important to a backpacker and that is map reading. It's a skill worth learning. A trip cannot be planned or executed properly without the aid of a map.

• **U.S.G.S. Topo** For wilderness areas the best available maps are the topographical maps prepared by the U.S. Geological Survey. These show roads, trails, water courses, lakes, forest cover, works of man and elevations. By a system of contour lines they also show surface configuration with a sense of three-dimensional relief.

Topographical maps come in a number of different sizes and scales but the most useful one for the backpacker is probably the 15-minute quadrangle. This map covers 15 minutes of latitude and longitude, an area of about 13 by 17 miles, at a scale of 1 : 62,500 or approximately 1 inch to a mile, with a contour interval of 80 feet. It's as adequate a representation of terrain as one could wish for. With this size and scale of map you can plan the route and pick likely campsites for your trip with some foresight and accuracy. Combined with a reliable guidebook, a detailed picture emerges of the overall trip.

Map study at home also increases your range of alternative moves once you're into the trip. This can be important in emergency situations, or if you decide to vary your original plan. A topographical map can also be handy for accurate noncompass orientation, which consists of matching up the map with recognized landmarks around you. In any case, the more you know about the country you're in the better off you are.

Altogether, maps are a beautiful expression of the human intelligence, especially these topo maps of the U.S.G.S. with their interesting combination of verbal, symbolic, and graphic means to describe what is wild. In addition, they have the characteristic of being verifiable in some detail—they tell you that someplace will be there when you get there and that it will look pretty much as indicated, which is comforting in a world such as ours. For the backpacker the topo map can become an expression of space-time relations in a very futuristic mode—it is a book and a picture that you can walk through.

Once into wilderness you will learn the final lesson of a map—no map will show everything and not everything will be as it appears on the map.

- **Where to Get Topo Maps** U.S. Geological Survey maps are available at most stores specializing in outdoor equipment. Maps in the 15-minute series usually sell for $1.25 each. You can also order them directly from the U.S.G.S. map distribution section for your area. Maps covering the area east of the Mississippi River can be ordered from: Branch of Distribution, U.S. Geological Survey, 1200 South Eads Street, Arlington, Virginia 22202. For maps of the area west of the Mississippi: Branch of Distribution, U.S. Geological Survey, Federal Center, Lakewood, Colorado 80225. For Alaska: Distribution Section, U.S. Geological Survey, 310 First Avenue, Fairbanks, Alaska 99701.

The U.S.G.S. also has map distribution offices which sell maps over-the-counter only. They will, however, mail you an index map of the state or area you are interested in, free of charge. The

index map shows the state or area divided into quadrangles. Each quadrangle is a separate map and has a name. Find the one or more quads that cover your area of interest and order them by name. These map distribution offices are located in the following cities: Washington, D.C.; Dallas, Texas; Salt Lake City, Utah; Spokane, Washington; Menlo Park, Los Angeles and San Francisco, California; Denver, Colorado; Reston, Virginia; Rolla, Missouri; and Anchorage and Juneau, Alaska.

The index map includes a list of retail outlets that carry U.S.G.S. maps. A booklet describing topographic maps and symbols is also available free on request. Some public libraries and many college and university libraries maintain collections of U.S.G.S. maps.

• **Canadian Topo Maps** In Canada maps from the National Topographical Series, the equivalent of the U.S.G.S. topos, are available from: Canada Map Office, Department of Energy, Mines and Resources, 615 Booth Street, Ottawa, Ontario, Canada K1A OE9.

• **U.S. Forest Service Maps** The U.S. Forest Service issues maps of the national forests, all of which contain large areas of wilderness, in addition to more accessible recreational areas. They are base maps and do not give the contour of the land, but aside from this, they give just about as much information as the U.S.G.S. topo maps. Because they are revised more frequently than the topo, the information about roads and trails is more up-to-date. An index map and any one map per order are free; additional maps cost 50 cents each. They are available at all regional offices of the U.S. Forest Service (U.S. Department of Agriculture), and forest ranger stations in the field.

• **Fish and Game Maps** The Fish and Game Departments of the various states are often another source of maps and literature covering backcountry. In California, for example, a series of "Angler's Guides" is published by the Department of Fish and Game. Each guide covers an area and has a representational map which clearly shows the waters and trails of the area. The text describes all fishing waters in a concise, informative way.

• **How to Fold Map** It's convenient to consult a map without having to unfold the whole map to get to the part you want, especially in a wind. The U.S.G.S. topo map is best folded in the following

24

manner. Fold the map in half along the east-west center line, with the map face out. Then make a vertical accordian fold into four equal panels so that the quadrangle name in the northeast corner of the map is visible on what will be the top panel. This is a good home use and filing size. To make it pocket size, accordian fold along east-west lines into four smaller panels so that the quadrangle name will still be visible on the top panel.

COMPASS

Another kind of reading to learn before venturing into wilderness is compass reading. A compass is one of those things that you rarely use in fact, but would feel less than well equipped without. If you have a map and are being fairly attentive to it and to the country you're passing through, whether by trail or cross-country, there is really not much need for a compass. But it would be necessary to have one in unmapped or feature-poor country, or when low visibility blots out the landscape.

Compasses are handy also for odd things like orienting your campsite to catch the morning sun, or just wanting to know apropos of nothing which way north lies. It's been known to quell jitters just to know where north lies, and to know that you are the center from which all directions proceed. The Chinese, who invented the compass, first used the magnetic needle for divination. The compass orients in relation to the direction of earth's magnetism.

There are two different types of compass. One, the sighting compass, will have an accurate hairline sighting device of some kind, usually with a mirror or lens arrangement to give degree reading while sighting. The other kind will have a less elaborate sighting device, a simple sighting line or arrow. The elaborate sighting compass is generally more than is required on a backpacking trip.

An adequate compass for backpacking will have the azimuth reading clockwise from zero to 360 degrees. It will have a well-magnetized needle, pivoted on a jewel bearing, in a liquid-filled clear plastic case housed in aluminum. The liquid will dampen needle oscillation quickly—within four seconds—making a steadier needle. The transparent base, with plainly marked sighting arrow, will rotate for easy sighting. One of the beauties of such a compass is that it can be placed directly on the map and read through the case. It will have luminous points for reading at night.

With this basic compass you should be able to determine direction, do sightings, take bearings, and orient maps with ease. Even if you never have to do these things, it's a good idea to learn how to do them just in case. Also learn how to correct for declination, which is the difference between the true north of the north star and magnetic north.

Most compasses are sold with detailed instructions on their use.

CLUBS AND FRIENDS

One other way to prepare for backpacking would be to join a club that promotes outdoor life. There are very large clubs like the Sierra Club and the Appalachian Trail Conference. Then there are innumerable local trail and hiking clubs. For some, an organized group outing, like those sponsored by the Sierra Club, may be the best introduction to backpacking in wilderness. Others of a loner temperament may want to work it out themselves. An ideal arrangement between these two extremes would be a friend who knows wilderness backpacking, is willing to teach you the preliminaries and perhaps take you on your first outing. For a list of some leading outdoor clubs, see pages 186-187.

PERMITS

Best take care of these before you go.

• **Camping Permit** A permit is required for all National Forest Wilderness and Primitive Areas. Obtainable at local and field Forest Service offices. For National Parks, permits are available from local or field National Park Service offices. This is also your campfire permit. Free.

In some heavily used National Park and National Forest Wilderness areas daily entry quotas have been set up at the trailheads. If you suspect the area you will be going to is under a quota system, best find out about it. To make sure you don't arrive at a trailhead only to find its quota filled for the day, you should make a reservation by mail for that trailhead, for that date. Write the Ranger Station or Entrance Station nearest the trailhead you will be leaving from. It's also a good idea to check for high fire danger areas where building fires may be temporarily prohibited.

• **Fishing License** Most outdoor sporting goods stores sell these.

27

THE OUTFIT

Equipment should be judged on qualities such as durability, weight and performance. How well does it do the things it's supposed to do? A clumsy, shoddily made piece of equipment is a burden in wilderness where breakdown and malfunction can be a real problem. Equipment must feel right, which is a part of its design, the aesthetic of the matter, if you will. Why not say that equipment should be both right and beautiful, the most elegant solution of a need? Let it be neither more nor less than it has to be to do its job.

In this chapter we are concerned primarily with an outfit for temperate zone, spring to autumn trips into wilderness. Essentially, we want a basic outfit to which other items can be added according to personal needs and the needs of any particular trip. We also want an outfit that will be adequate in the widest range of conditions. Fortunately, mountain, forest and desert wilderness require much the same basic outfit.

We will be covering equipment in some detail, on the premise that if your equipment is squared away before you go into wilderness, you won't have to fuss over it once you're there.

CLOTHES

First, let's try to work out the ideal set of clothes. Though you should choose each item for its own qualities, you should also think about how it will combine with the other items of your set. Again you want to carry the minimum set of clothes that will serve over the widest range of conditions.

We have stated the weight of clothes recommended in this chapter. Most good equipment catalogs give the weight of all items in a complete outfit.

What do we ask of clothes? In the ideal climate we would be happiest lightly clothed or naked. Being warm-blooded creatures, however, whatever the climate we must maintain an internal temperature of around 98.6°F. Heat circulates through the body by way of the blood stream. When it gets hot, from weather or exertion, there is vaso-dilation, and the blood circulates excess heat away from the vital organs to surface tissue and the extremities. When it gets cold, vaso-constriction reduces the blood supply to surface tissue and extremities in order to conserve the heat of the vital organs. Thus the ideal set of clothes will allow us to ventilate heat away in warm weather and conserve body heat in the cold.

Clothes are such a personal item, however, that there can be no final word on them. Individual heat and cold tolerance varies too much to set down any general rules for clothes. Only by getting out into wilderness and experimenting will you find the set of clothes that best suits you. What follows are suggestions and possibilities, starting from the inside and working out.

UNDERWEAR

You may either get a set of special underwear or improvise some other combination. If you are going into country you know to be cold, not only mornings and evenings but through the day, it would be wise to consider a set of long underwear.

The most efficient underwear is the open-mesh or fishnet type. The principle here is to trap warm air next to the body in the mesh pockets, and at the same time allow body moisture to evaporate out. This is vital because your body perspires constantly. Even without exertion, it gives off a pint of water every eight hours in breath and fine perspiration.

Fishnet underwear comes in cotton, or wool-and-cotton combination. It has the disadvantage of not working unless it's under something, and by itself it won't keep insects off.

Then there are the traditional wool or cotton long johns. These unfortunately don't ventilate well, and so with the slightest exertion you begin

to sweat in them. The sweat isn't evaporated but wicked right into the fabric and wet underwear doesn't have much insulating power. Don't take the whole set if you can get along with either the top or the bottom separately.

Instead of underwear, a cotton T-shirt may serve your needs, or a long-sleeved cotton turtle-neck or crew-neck shirt. These, of course, may serve as outer shirts, too.

SHIRTS

Possibilities here include a cotton or light wool (about 10-ounce-weight fabric) shirt with long sleeves, long tail, buttoned-flap breast pockets, and buttons all the way down the front; or the afore-mentioned cotton turtle- or crew-neck shirt, rib knit or jersey. Long sleeves keep off insects and a buttoned front makes the shirt adjustable. Think of the type of shirt that gives you the most com-fort while working. Think of the kind of weather you're likely to meet.

PANTS

For extended walking in rugged country, loose-fitting pants are best. In hiking your legs are the most active part of your body and need cooling. Tight-legged pants tend to bind in the crotch and legs, especially if you have sweat into them, or have been caught by rain. On the other hand, some people feel their snug fit to be a comfort. Be sure pockets are strong. At least one back pocket should button down. Watch pockets are handy. Cuffs are useless. A light but tough twill fabric (like whipcord), either cotton or wool backed with synthetics, is the standard material for a good pair of outdoor pants.

Many backpackers swear by walking shorts. These, too, should be of a generous cut. If you don't want to take both pants and shorts, a pair of pants can be fixed so they will convert to shorts. Find a pair of wide-legged pants. Then draw the pant legs up inside themselves and hold with snaps or buttons. Don't forget a belt to keep your pants where you want them and to hang things from, but don't overload it. Or how about suspenders?

SWEATER, HEAVY WOOL SHIRT, DOWN JACKET OR DOWN VEST

Through the day you're likely to be in shirt and pants, your first layer of insulation. In the cold of morning and night you'll want a garment that is heavier or has more insulating power. This is your second layer of insulation.

• **Sweater** A light, fuzzy, open-weave, wool sweater or a heavier, bulky-knit, Icelandic one could fill the bill. But the light sweater may be too light against sustained cold, while the Icelandic, though warm, may be too heavy or too bulky for packing. Clothes are a compromise at best. A pullover is not very adjustable. If it gets too hot, all you can do is take it off. If it gets cold, you can put a shell parka over it to increase its efficiency somewhat. Perhaps the most you can say for a well-made sweater is that it has esthetic appeal.

• **Heavy Wool Shirt** More efficient as second-layer insulation would be a medium-to-heavy wool shirt (14- to 20-ounce-weight fabric), with all the features enumerated for the light shirt. It's more efficient than a sweater because it's more adjustable to changing conditions. If it gets too warm, you can unbutton the front, roll up the sleeves, or pull out the tail, depending on the degree of ventilation you want. If it gets cold, you can button up, tuck in the tail, and pull up the collar. A heavy shirt can also be combined with a shell parka for more warmth. A well-made shirt of about 20-ounce weight, 100 percent pure virgin wool fabric with its thick soft nap is a beautiful garment to wear. Twill

or diagonal weave makes a strong fabric. Wool nap has great insulating and water-shedding qualities, and unlike any other fabric, doesn't feel clammy when wet. In fact, even when wet it continues to give warmth. A heavy wool shirt does, however, have the disadvantage of weight and bulk.

• **Light Down Jacket** Strictly from the point of view of efficiency—warmth per weight and bulk—nothing beats a waterfowl down garment. A light down jacket weighs from 16 to 20 ounces, as compared to 26 ounces for a heavy wool shirt. It has the advantage of compressibility: It will stuff into a sack about 3 by 8 inches. Above all, it will provide all the warmth you'll need on a back-packing trip.

The ideal down jacket will have a nylon zipper down the front covered by a snap-down flap which allows closure with zipper open; elastic cuffs with snaps for better ventilation control at the wrist; a drawstring around the bottom for vertical air-flow control; a down-filled collar that snaps

under the chin to cut off air movement about the neck; and a couple of down-filled pockets for warming hands. The collar should accept a snap-on hood.

The insulation of down jackets depends on loft—the volume to which the down can expand. The ideal down jacket will be filled with about 9 ounces of down and have a thickness or loft of at least 1-1/2 inches. A jacket of this type breathes well, allowing moisture to escape, while retaining body heat as insulation.

As in all down articles the outer fabric must be light and soft enough to allow the down to expand to its full loft, and at the same time be resistant to wear. Nylon is the preferred fabric for its strength and lightness. A fabric of about 2-ounce weight is generally used.

The disadvantages of a down jacket are the difficulty of drying it out if it gets wet through, and the weakness of nylon against fire damage—even a small coal popping out of a fire can burn right through nylon fabric.

• **Down Parka** This is essentially the light down jacket lengthened to extend over the hips. The extra length assures warmth over the lower back and prevents back ride-up of jacket when active. Look for cargo pocket (with flap closure) super-

imposed on insulated hand-warmer pocket. In addition, it should have all the features enumerated for the light down jacket above.

• **Down Vest** If you took the light down jacket and cut off its sleeves, you would be left with the down vest. The idea of the vest is to keep your torso warm. If the torso with its vital organs is kept warm, heat will not be called in from the extremities and you'll feel warm all over. The vest should be cut longer by 3 inches in back to cover ride-up when you bend over.

SHELL PARKA

The shell parka is the windproof, water-repellent layer of your set of clothes. To work properly, insulating clothes must be able to breathe out body moisture. But clothes that breathe are subject to wind and rain penetration. The shell parka is designed to give some protection against wind and rain, but in order to do its job right it must itself breathe, or body moisture would be captured and condense on its inside surface. In other words, a parka can't be perfectly windproof, it can only be more windproof—of more tightly woven fabric—than the clothes it covers. For the same reason, it can't be waterproof. It will repel water for a short time and then soak through. It is mainly protection against dry, windy cold.

Shell parkas come in light and heavier weights. For summer backpacking the light shell parka, a garment weighing about a pound, will do. Ideally it should be fingertip length and have a hood. The fabric (about 2-1/2-ounce nylon, or now more generally 60/40 cloth—60 percent cotton, 40 percent nylon) should be double layered through

the upper sleeves, upper body and hood. For good adjustability it should have a two-way nylon zipper down front that opens from top and bottom, and a snap-fastened overlap. The zipper should close up to chin level. The hood should have a drawstring around the front to adjust the face opening. A drawcord inside the waist and a closure system for the cuffs (snaps, buttons, or velcro tabs) gives added ventilation control. It should have a couple of breast pockets and a couple of large combination cargo/hand-warmer pockets at the hips. The pockets should be zippered or fixed with velcro closures. Some parkas come furnished with a zippered compartment across the back, a very handy extra space.

PONCHO

This is the wonderfully versatile and essential piece of equipment that waterproofs your outfit. A poncho is made of either sheet plastic or nylon fabric coated with rubber or plastic. Basically, it's a rectangle of waterproof material with a hole in the center for the head to go through, and a hood fixed around the hole to cover the head. It simply drapes over you like a tent. Snap closures are set along the side.

The poncho covers both you and your pack should you be caught by rain on the trail. With it on, you can keep walking, or stop and crouch under it till the weather clears. It can be pitched as an emergency shelter. At night it can be used as a ground cloth under your sleeping bag. If your shell parka proves inadequate in a biting cold wind, the poncho will give the needed extra protection. Its very loose closure system allows good ventilation control.

Someday you will want to have a good poncho. The sheet-plastic ponchos, though inexpensive, just don't stand up to hard use. They tend to stiffen, crack and tear as they weather. The ideal poncho would be made of light but strong nylon fabric (about 2-1/2-ounce weight) coated with a tough plastic resin—a fabric that will remain pliant even in cold. Ponchos are now made in two sizes, standard (84 by 70 inches) and pack-frame (100 by 70 inches). The pack-frame size is designed to cover both you and your pack and still fall low enough to give some protection to the back of your legs—something that a standard poncho does inadequately. The pack-frame size seems indicated. It has snaps down each side, grommets set in the corners and a hood with a drawstring. For better ventilation control and ease in putting it on, a zipper at the neck may be included.

OUTDOOR FABRIC BREAKTHROUGH

One thing we've lacked in outdoor equipment is a truly satisfactory waterproof fabric for outerwear clothes. We do have waterproof fabrics, for instance, fabrics coated with urethane, a synthetic rubber. But urethane-coated fabrics don't breathe.

The basic problem is that a fabric that doesn't breathe will condense body moisture vapor on its inside surface. For this reason, fabrics used in outdoor outerwear clothes are generally made water repellant rather than waterproof. This is a compromise solution because, while a water-repellant fabric breathes, it can only shed water to a point before soaking through.

The ideal waterproof outerwear fabric would have the seemingly contradictory properties of being impermeable to liquid water while at the same time being permeable to water vapor (perspiration). We now have such a fabric. Gore-tex laminate. Gore-tex is a microporous membrane of polytetrafluorethylene. It has about nine billion pores per square inch. Water droplets are much too large to penetrate the pores, but water vapor will readily diffuse through them. Gore-tex is laminated to fabrics. Gore-tex laminate fabrics will revolutionize outdoor outerwear clothes and equipment. It is not yet widely available, but look for it when buying clothes and equipment.

HEAD TO TOE
• **Hat** The head is the only extremity where blood supply is never reduced. Since it has no vaso-constriction mechanism, it receives a constant supply of blood regardless of changes in heat and cold. Because of this, it radiates more heat than any other part of the body. Thus, covering your head when it's cold will help heat the rest of the body. When it's hot, uncovering the head will help cool the body.

There are varieties of headgear. For cold, a wool-knit watch cap would be adequate. A balaclava, a knit hood which covers the entire head, might be considered for the protection it gives the neck. In hot weather, whatever you put on your head to keep off the sun should have good air circulation.

- **Bandanna** This is always a handy item especially for improvising headgear. Large size is best.
- **Mittens** Consider wool mittens or gloves for early- and late-season trips to the mountains.
- **Rain Chaps** These are like cowboy's chaps but are made of coated nylon, small in bulk and lightweight. They make walking in rain or through wet brush possible without soaking pants. Worth carrying if you know there's high probability of rain where you are going. (4 ounces)
- **Cagoule** The cagoule is a very large, loose-fitting sack with hood and sleeves made of waterproof coated nylon. It is generally knee length and cut wide at the hem. Not a very versatile garment but useful perhaps in a bivouac situation. Its main drawback is that strenuous activity with it on would, of course, bathe you in sweat. A short cagoule (to just below the hips) is called an anorak. It has the same disadvantage as the cagoule.
- **Socks** There are two general types of outdoor sock, the traditional, heavy, wool Ragg-knit sock and the newer terry-stitch sock. The Ragg-knit sock has the cushion and warmth of wool, but the rough weave tends to be uncomfortable next to the skin and may require an inner sock. This type also tends to get out of shape with wear, and so you may have the problem of wrinkling which can be unpleasant while hiking.

In summertime the terry-stitch sock would seem to be better. The stretchable terry-stitch creates air pockets for insulation and gives cushion and softness at the same time; an inner sock isn't necessary and the stretch stitch prevents wrinkling. The terry-stitch is also designed to wick moisture from the inner to the outer layer of the sock to keep the feet dry—relatively dry. There is no combination of sock and boot that will keep feet perfectly dry while hiking. The medium weight (3-1/2 ounces per pair), synthetic fiber and cotton combination would seem to be a good choice for summer hiking. The brand name is Wick-Dri.

There is also a wool terry-stitch thermal sock. In addition to extra warmth, it has all the advantages of the terry-stitch and none of the disadvantages of the Ragg.

BOOTS

Since backpacking is walking, be good to your feet. Any kind of footwear not designed specifically for hiking generally turns out wanting in one feature or another. A good trip into wilderness depends so much on being well shod. It can be miserable like nothing else to hike with an ill-fitting boot. If once into wilderness your boot starts hurting, there's nothing to do but endure the pain for the rest of the trip.

For the kind of backpacking we've been speaking of, a light trail boot or a medium-weight hiking boot seems right. The heavy mountaineering boot is more boot than necessary. There is currently a tendency among backpackers to be overshod. It's good to remember that the Indian walked most of the trails now in use barefoot or with moccasins. For trail hiking, as well as for moderate to rough cross-country, the light trail boot is perfectly adequate. In fact, people who use the even lighter low-cut leather athletic shoe report them to be fairly adequate outback. They require that you step more carefully than with a boot, but that is no true disadvantage. Many people carry both a pair of boots and a pair of these light athletic shoes.

It is time we had a hiking shoe lighter than the light trail boot, but as supportive. A shoe about as light as the leather basketball shoe, yet tough enough for the backcountry. Current shoe technology is capable of delivering such a shoe. In fact, Adidas has come very close with their light, leather, high-top hiking boot, Zurs. They weigh just 36 ounces per pair (size 8).

The light trail boot is the lightest traditional mountain boot we have that is adequate for back-

packing. But then some people prefer the medium-weight boot. The question of light or heavy at the foot is a matter of personal preference. Some people like to be heavily shod, and some lightly. There's a wide variety of boots available in both light and medium weights, and your choice will, of course, depend on more factors than could ever be contained in a rule. A well-made boot, however, should incorporate certain basic features.

A light trail boot shouldn't weigh more than 3-1/2 pounds; a medium-weight boot will weigh about 4 pounds. Both will be about 6 inches high, enough to cover ankles. The leather should be strong enough to resist rock abrasion—either rough-out (not suede) or smooth finish. The boot should be waterproof, or almost so—a boot must breathe some to be comfortable. It should be lined with smooth, soft leather, and be padded around the ankle for comfort, support, warmth and protection against side-rock bruising. The padding also helps to hold the heel in place so that it doesn't

slip and chafe. The tongue should be padded too, for comfort and to keep it from bunching. Gussets should be attached to the tongue and rise nearly to the top of the boot to keep out water and dirt. A padded collar around the top is good for keeping out pebbles, but if too tight may cut down on ventilation. The toe cap and heel counter should be reinforced. The fewer seams the better. For lacing, some boots have eyelets and others have hooks—a matter of personal preference. Braided nylon laces that are waxed seem most trouble free. The rubber lug sole such as Vibram is best for hiking. The sole of the medium-weight boot should be extra secured with brass screws.

• **Fitting the Boot** The best way to buy boots is to go to a store and try them on till you find the right pair for you. Salespeople in mountain stores are generally very helpful. When fitting, keep the following basic points in mind. Remember that the boot must support your own weight as well as the weight of your pack; when you put on a boot try to imagine by its feel the way it will adjust to the extra load. (It would be a good idea for stores to have a 30-pound pack handy in the boot department so this could be tested right there.) Remember, too, that boots are stiff and that they've been packed flat in their carton. With use they will shape to your foot. Don't pay too much attention to numbered size; attend carefully to the actual fit.

Put on the sock you intend to wear with the boot. To check toe room, stand up in the unlaced boot and push your toes forward as far as they will go. If your middle finger just slides into the space left at the heel, you know your toe room is right. Now slide foot back and lace the boot firmly all the way up, especially across the instep. If it feels loose around the instep, take into account the stiffness of the new boot. Standing with your weight even on both feet, wiggle your toes and pull them back toward the foot; there should be room for free toe movement. To test the fit across the ball of the foot and at the heel, have someone hold the boot firmly at the toe and heel while you stand on that foot and twist it from side to side. The ball of the foot should feel snug and hardly move; the heel should not move side to side at all. Now walk with boots laced firmly—still keeping in mind the stiffness of a new boot. If your heel moves up and down very loosely, the fit isn't right. The boot is too long, or it's too wide at the heel. Now knock the toe of the boot against the floor, or hook the heel on something and push forward. Your foot shouldn't slip forward, and your toes shouldn't hit the front of the boot or feel pinched. If they do, the boot is either too short or too narrow.

Take your time fitting. When you get a boot that feels right, try a size smaller and a size larger to make sure. A proper store will have an exchange privilege; ask about the conditions of it so there is no misunderstanding. Catalogs include instructions on how to order boots by mail—a risky thing to do at best.

• **Breaking in Boots** A medium-weight boot will require some breaking in. The gradual method is always best. Start by wearing the boots around the house, and then take longer walks. Always wear them with socks you're planning to wear on the trip. If you run short of time, the approved crash method is to soak them in water overnight and walk them dry the next day. In any case, be sure your boots are well broken in before you go on your trip.

• **Boot Care** Immediately after buying a new boot, apply a wax waterproofing like Sno-Seal. Either warm the boot or melt the wax a little for good penetration, and rub in vigorously. Grease and oils are said to make the leather stretch. Leath-R-Seal is good for waterproofing seams and welt (the strip between sole and top). After use, when dirt cakes into the wax, saddle soap the boot before applying fresh waterproofing. It doesn't hurt a good boot to get wet, but dry them slowly. Walking a boot dry seems best. Never put boots close to a fire to dry. The heat parches the leather and can make the sole curl up.

• **Camp Shoe or Slipper** At the end of the hiking day, it's great to take off the boots and put on slippers to pad around the camp. Rubber thongs might do, but cold mornings and evenings are when you need slippers.

• **Down Booties** For those with chill feet, down booties are definitely the answer. They are fabric double shell, in the form of a boot, filled with down or synthetic fiberfill. The ensolite sole, for insulation, is covered with tough waterproof fabric. These could substitute for slippers.

PACK

For backpacking two types of pack may be considered adequate: the framed rucksack and the pack-frame assembly.

FRAMED RUCKSACK

The main advantage of the rucksack is its low center of gravity. Most generally it is used for shorter trips, or for trips that involve extra rough cross-country climbing or skiing—any place where balance and free movement of arms, shoulders and head are important. It could even be used on a longer backpacking trip. With judicious planning and packing, it can easily hold supplies for a week or more.

The frame is part of the internal structure of the rucksack. It serves to hold the pack in shape and keep it away from the wearer's back, allowing air to circulate for coolness. The top of the pack is supposed to hang slightly away from the back, which is one of its disadvantages—the pack tends to pull backwards on the shoulders. A backward pull can be uncomfortable with a heavy load, and the energy used to resist it is needlessly wasted.

In any carrying system, the less you have to lean forward with a load on your back, the more comfortable you are and the less energy you waste.

Since we walk upright and not on all fours, we can't carry weight on our back like a mule or burro. In carrying a pack we can either suspend the weight of it from the top of our shoulders, or somehow transfer the weight of it to our hips. The rucksack is essentially a shoulder-suspended carrying system. It has the aforementioned disadvantage of pulling back on the wearer's shoulders, and also puts a vertical crush on the spine which tires all of the back.

Lately there's been an attempt to combine the rucksack with a suspension system that transfers load weight to the hips as in the pack-frame assembly. Basically, it is the rucksack with internal frame attached to a padded waist-belt. Instead of having a padded waist-belt, some rucksacks will extend out and pad their lower inside corners to form a belt. This wrap-around design holds the pack directly to the body. The argument for this design is that the pack is held closer to the wearer's center of gravity so that just a slight lean forward regains the wearer's balance. This can be a great advantage when doing rough cross-country, or any activity where maintaining balance is important. To be up-to-date, any rucksack should have an internal frame and some system of transferring weight from the shoulders to the hips via a waist-belt of some kind. Framed rucksacks will weigh from 3-1/2 to 4-1/2 pounds.

PACK-FRAME ASSEMBLY

The pack and frame weigh approximately 4 pounds. The pack-frame assembly is designed to put the load high and close to the back, so that with a minimal forward lean of the body, the center of gravity is placed directly over the hips. The load bearing is then transferred at the the hips, by means of a waist-belt, to the legs, which are the most muscular part of our bodies and meant by nature to bear weight. The top of the pack tips forward and is wedged against the back by the shoulder harness. This action is designed to hold the load close to the body for stability and to prevent backward pull.

• **Frame** A good frame will be made of aluminum or magnesium aircraft tubing, heli-arc welded together. The rigidity of this frame is both the weakness and the strength of a pack-frame assembly—it won't have the "give" of a rucksack, but will carry a load more efficiently. Magnesium, which is lighter than aluminum but just as strong, is now used more and more. The frame should "s" curve slightly to fit the back, and, as previously mentioned, rise high to place the load over the hips and legs with a small forward lean of the body. The cross-bracing bars should curve outward to clear the back. The frame should rest against the back on a nylon-mesh panel. The shoulder straps should be padded. They should be broad at the shoulder for weight distribution and then taper to clear the arms. The all-important waist-belt should also be padded; it must be comfortable because it holds a major part of the load.

Some frames will have two light, vertical rods up the center of the frame to protect the back

from sharp objects in the pack. For attaching the pack to the frame some arrangement of clevis pins or eyebolts is generally used. Some pack-frame assemblies allow for the pack to be moved up or down on the frame, depending on whether a high or low center of gravity is desired. The high position is best for easy hiking trails, the low position for rough cross-country. Trailwise has such a pack.

To overcome the aforementioned rigidity of the arc-welded frame, JanSport has come up with a flexible frame obtained by means of mechanically secured joints. The idea is to retain the load-bearing advantage of the pack-frame assembly while gaining the flexibility of the rucksack. In addition, their hip-suspension system allows the base of the frame to cant outward during extreme ascents and descents. Thoughtful refinements both.

Another recent innovation in pack frames comes from Alpenlite. It is a wrap-around frame. The regular frame transfers the weight of the pack vertically, the wrap-around frame brings the weight of the pack to the hips at an angle. It is claimed that this method transfers the weight more evenly around the hips. Some may find the frame cumbersome (though it has elegant lines), but it does carry a load comfortably, which is the point.

The very latest in frames comes from North Face. It is a frame that allows hips and shoulders to move more or less independently of each other. This is accomplished by means of a flexible joint that takes the load of the pack and transfers it to the hips, not rigidly as in the usual frame-harness system, but with the possibility of a flexing motion according to how the body moves. The joint is placed at the small of the back, the point of

minimum cyclic motion in walking. It attaches to the waist-belt by means of a curved bar. The design eliminates tiring hip-shoulder torque strain transmitted through frame-harness under load. A fine innovation.

• **Pack** The pack comes in a great variety of styles. Ideally it should be made of 7-1/2- or 8-1/2-ounce coated waterproof nylon duck sewn with nylon or dacron thread. The general shape of the pack should be wide and thin. The average size of the 3/4-length pack is about 8 inches deep by 16 inches wide by 21 inches high. This basic sack may be undivided, or divided vertically or horizontally into two, three or more compartments. A divided sack makes for easy access to any part of the load without having to dig deep or empty out. North Face has a pack with a zippered back panel that opens out the entire pack. Most packs have pockets attached to each side and one on the back, with perhaps a map pocket on the flap, all with covered nylon-zipper closures. The 3/4-length pack attaches to the top of the frame with room underneath for strapping on the sleeping bag. Pack-frame assemblies come in different sizes (small, medium, large) so be sure you get a proper fit.

• **How To Stow It** The general rule is to stow the heavy part of the load close to your back and high, but not so high as to make the pack top-heavy. Light things should go to the bottom and away from your back. The side and rear pockets are best for items you want quick to hand. A properly loaded pack will neither pull you back nor push you forward. On a backpacking trip you usually repack your bag each day. Take some care doing it; it will make a difference in your walking.

SLEEPING BAG

Until very recently, the only sleeping bag worth considering for backpacking was the goose down bag. Now, with the advent of polyester fiberfills like Dacron II and Polarguard, the synthetic-filled sleeping bag approaches somewhat closer to the quality and efficiency of the down bag. Synthetic fillers don't have the lightness and the loft per pound of down, nor down's compressibility, but they are tougher, cheaper and have virtues like drying quickly when wet and maintaining loft and warmth even when wet. And though they may not have the loft per pound of down, they hold what loft they have as well or better than down. Their drawbacks are weight and bulk. A synthetic-filled bag is about half again as heavy as an equivalent down bag, and perhaps a fifth or more as bulky when stuffed. These are not such outrageous drawbacks when you think of it. But, despite its comparative fragility and expense, the down bag is still the premier bag for backpacking. Why down?

As discussed in the section on clothes, any down article works by conserving the natural heat of the body. This requires somehow wrapping the body with a layer of insulation to prevent the heat from escaping. Air would be a perfect insulator because of its zero weight and high nonconductivity, except that it moves and could carry away the natural body heat. However, air tends to stick to a surface to a distance of about 1/8 inch out from that surface. Any material that stops air movement at 1/8-inch intervals or less will create an insulating layer.

Goose down is just such a material. Its light, fluffy structure is ideal for trapping air and creating insulating space. It also satisfies the backpacker's need for lightness: An ounce of good down will fill about 600 cubic inches and compress under hand pressure to only 15 cubic inches. After being compressed, even for great lengths of time, it has the power of re-expanding to its original volume. Being a natural substance, down's cellular structure absorbs and dispels excess body moisture.

DESIGN

Bags come in different sizes and shapes. Take care to find the right fit for your body. For the backpacker, the close-fitting mummy bag would seem the first choice. It is light, compact and very efficient in conserving heat. If a mummy bag seems too constricting for you, a larger semirectangular bag would be in order. A heavy-bodied or claustrophobic person would probably feel most comfortable in a bag of this type. However, a larger bag will be heavier and have more space to heat, and generally it won't have a hood. Ultimately it's a matter of compromising between space and warmth. A light mummy will weigh from 2-1/2 to just over 3 pounds; a semirectangular will weigh 4 pounds and more.

• **Construction** Down is held between an inner shell and a larger outer shell, employing the same insulating principle as the thermos bottle. This allows the down to expand evenly around the bag and prevents the sleeper from pushing through the inner layer to the outer shell. In connecting the two shells no seams should be sewn through the bag, as this would create uninsulated cold spots. Instead both inner and outer shells should be held together by baffles which are sewn around the circumference of the bag to form lateral tubes. These stop the down from shifting over the length of the bag. The baffles should not be more than 6 inches apart; bags using a lengthwise baffle system should be avoided. Baffles are sewn in several different ways, the most efficient and widely used ones being: slant wall, box tube, overlapping V-tube and the chevron. Although each has its adherents, all are essentially the same in practice.

• **Fabric** Tightly woven nylon fabric of about 1.5-ounce weight or slightly heavier is generally used for lightweight bags. The weave must be tight enough so that the down won't leak through. It also should be water repellent, abrasion resistant and rip proof. It must be light enough to allow the down to achieve its maximum loft. Nylon may seem like a sleazy material for wilderness, but it has its own considerable virtue. Although it is cold to the touch, it warms very quickly and absorbs less heat from the body than cotton flannel.

• **Down and Loft** Loft is the most important indicator of a bag's warmth. It is measured as total thickness through the bag as it lies on the ground. But loft is a tricky matter. For a bag to loft to its full potential, just the right amount of down for the amount of space must be used; more than necessary is a waste. A good bag will not feel overstuffed with down. The amount of down will vary with the size and shape of the bag. A semi-rectangular bag will average around 35 ounces of down, a very light mummy, around 26 ounces. Both will deliver an appropriate 6 inches of loft.

A light bag with a 6-inch loft will generally be advertised as good to a minimum temperature of 10°F above zero. With proper ventilation control, a bag like this will be comfortable even to 60°F. On extra-warm nights, open it out flat and sleep under it. Finally, in choosing the weight of your bag, consider the amount of covering you normally use. In other words, do you sleep hot or cold?

• **Zipper** The zipper gets you in and out of your bag, and is important also in ventilation control. Nylon, self-lubricating zippers are best. The zipper should have two double-toggle sliders that allow it to be opened both from the top and the bottom—a great advantage for ventilation control. The whole length of the zipper should be covered inside the bag by a down-filled tube. A bag that zips down the center or just half way down the side is less flexible than bags with a full-length, two-slider zipper. Mummy bags should zip all the way down one side or at least 70 inches. Semirectangular bags should have a two-slider zipper that runs all the way down one side and across the foot, so that the bag can be opened out flat. Only bags with full-length zippers can be zipped together to form double bags.

• **Hood** At the head of a mummy, the bottom half of the bag extends past the top. This extra length turns into a hood when the head opening is closed by means of a drawcord. When it's cold, and you're zipped and hooded in your bag, nothing need be exposed but your nose. A semirectangular bag suffers for not having a hood arrangement, although some have a drawcord closure at the head.

BAG CARE

The down sleeping bag, like so much we owe to modern technology, is durable yet at the same time

delicate and extremely vulnerable to damage. It wants care.

On a trip, as soon as you get up, shake the bag and spread it out over a branch or large rock—not on the ground. Always let it air and sun before stuffing it away. If you can't do this in the morning, do it along the trail during a break or at lunchtime. The bag will feel much better that night for your trouble.

A down bag must be kept dry. Never lay it directly on the ground where moisture can get at it. If you run into rain—before you do anything else—make sure that your sleeping bag does not get wet. A down bag, once soaked through, will take days to dry out.

Watch for sparks flying from your cooking fire. Repair any hole immediately before you lose down. Sew it with thread or patch it with ripstop tape.

Back home, air and sun the bag thoroughly. Never store it in its stuff sack. Put it in a safe dry place where it can remain lofted out.

• **Cleaning the Bag** There's a considerable difference of opinion about cleaning a bag. It is generally agreed, however, that water and soap washing is easier on the bag, and on the down in particular, than dry cleaning. Regular dry-cleaning chemicals tend to wash out the natural oils of down and take away its lofting power. Dry cleaning also leaves an unpleasant smell on the bag as well as a slightly oily residue. If you must dry clean your bag, make sure the cleaner has experience with down bags, and that a mild natural petroleum solvent is being used.

With water and soap washing, some say hand wash. But a quality bag of strong interior construction and good fabric should not be harmed by machine washing. Use cold water with Woolite or some nondetergent soap in a front-loading machine. Then run the bag through a water extractor if one is available at your laundromat. Wet down is heavy and the baffling that holds the down isn't that strong, so be careful handling and carrying a wet bag. A down bag can be dried in a large commercial dryer at medium to low heat. Be sure bag is unzipped. Something like a tennis ball thrown in with bag will help the down to fluff.

A bathtub is best for washing a bag by hand. Wash and rinse two or three times. Sponge off dirty spots. Then gently squeeze out all excess water. Don't wring. It will still be dripping wet, so pick it up carefully and lay it out flat in the sun on

a meshed surface like a chaise longue. Don't hang it on a line. It will take several sunny days to dry thoroughly. Keep checking it and gently pull apart clumps of down. Don't worry, the down will dry out and be as fluffy as ever. A bag shouldn't be washed too often.

SLEEPING PAD

A pad under the bag is an integral part of the sleeping unit. It satisfies the need for comfort and insulation. Convoluted polyurethane foam is the most efficient material for a pad. It's an improvement over the air mattress, which has disadvantages of springing leaks and poor insulation. A 2-inch-thick foam pad insures a comfortable night no matter what kind of ground you lie down on.

Sleeping pads come in a variety of sizes, but are generally 21 inches wide and anywhere from 38 to 76 inches long. Make your choice after considering such factors as the amount of bulk and weight you want to carry, and how comfortable you want to be at night. This kind of pad should be covered because the foam will absorb moisture. A cotton cover on top and coated, waterproof nylon on the

bottom is best. (The cotton top discourages your sleeping bag from sliding around.) It is best carried rolled tightly and lashed to the top of the pack frame, or rolled around the sleeping-bag sack and strapped to the bottom of the frame.

Ensolite, a high-density, closed-cell foam, is another possibility. It is light, flexible and waterproof. It provides excellent insulation. Generally sold in a thickness of 3/8 inch, it is not as comfortable as 2-inch thick polyurethane foam.

How about polyurethane foam laminated to ensolite, for an all-season sleeping pad?

SLEEPING BAG COVER

This is a large sack that the sleeping bag slips into. The cover keeps off wind and dampness, making the bag warmer. The top is breathable ripstop nylon and the bottom is waterproof nylon, so the cover will serve as ground cloth and also keep your bag clean. It should have a zipper along one side and be at least 7 feet long and 40 inches wide. Corner grommets and drawcord top make it an emergency bivouac sack. A sleeping bag cover will weigh about 1 pound.

TENT?

For the kind of backpacking we speak of, a formal tent would, generally, be more shelter than is necessary. A tent would be required in sustained cold or snow, or in a region known for raw, inclement weather. One would be handy, too, in country where mosquitoes or biting flies are a major problem, or on a trip planned around having a base camp. The beauty of a tent is that it gives relief from continuous exposure to the elements. It can feel positively luxurious to step from windswept exposure into the secure, weather-tight space of a well-designed tent.

Besides the formal tent, the tube tent might be considered, and the tarp tent, the latter an extremely versatile piece of equipment.

FORMAL TENT

A two-man tent is generally large enough to hold three people in a pinch. It is probably most suitable for a two- or three-person trip. Such a tent should, first, be weatherproof, able to withstand a storm of fair severity. It must be of durable material and construction. To be waterproof from wet ground it must have a tub floor of coated fabric. It should cross-ventilate by means of adjustable vents, windows and door. All openings should be mosquito-netted to protect from insects, and door and windows should zipper for weather-tightness. The canopy, or roof, must breathe. A waterproof flysheet is necessary to cover the canopy when it rains. The tent should pitch fast in an uncomplicated fashion with a minimum of guy lines. The double A-frame pole system is now standard with better-made tents. Poles shock corded. Finally, the tent should have some esthetic worth. A well-designed tent can be a thing of beauty in a wild setting. (5-1/2 to 6-1/2 pounds)

TUBE TENT
This is simply a thin (.003 inch) polyethylene tube which is open at both ends, about 9 feet long, with a circumference of 8 feet in the one-man size, and 12 feet in the two-man size. The ridge is formed by passing a cord through the tent and securing the ends to trees or rocks. Your gear and you anchor the floor. A one-man tube tent weighs 19 ounces, a two-man, 35 ounces.

TARP TENT
You may start out with a simple sheet of poly-ethylene plastic and make do, but eventually you will want a tarp tent that has been designed and manufactured to specifications. These should include a dimension of at least 10 feet square, with grommets around the perimeter, and hang-ties here and there on the body of the tarp. The fabric should be around 2.5 ounce per square yard coated nylon.

The beauty of a tarp shelter is that it can be made to fit most any situation. You will want a tarp in wind or prolonged rain, as a hedge against threatening weather, or to keep off heavy dew. For example, you plan to start off hiking at dawn or earlier and you are in country with heavy morning dew. If you don't want to pack a dew-soaked sleeping bag, try sleeping under a tarp shelter the night before. It is a fine test of ingenuity to pitch a tarp tent to just the right shape for the weather and terrain. A 10-foot square tarp tent will weigh around 2 pounds.

Plastic sheets aren't as durable, but because of their low cost you might feel that they're worth it even if they last only a trip or two. More than .003-inch thickness isn't necessary. A 6- by 8-foot tarp would be more than enough for a one-man shelter. For a party of more than one, visualize the size tarp that will cover everyone in their sleeping bags, plus their equipment, with a margin all around. You can always get along with less room than you think.

• **Nylon Cord** To make a tarp shelter you will need cord. If the tarp lacks grommets, you will also need a device to attach the cord to the tarp. You can buy ready-made devices such as Visqueen clamps, adhesive vinyl tape with grommet set in one end or Versa-Ties. Then again, you can improvise. The idea is simple—you wrap a small object like a stone in the tarp several inches away from the edge and tie it off with the cord, and there is your attachment. Braided white 1/8-inch nylon cord of 550-pound test strength is good cord. It's handy for other things too. (50 feet weighs 3 ounces)

COOKING UTENSILS

POTS, ETC.

An outdoor cookpot should have a cover that may also serve as frying pan and plate. The number and size of pots depends on the number of people in the party, the kind of cooking you plan to do, and whether you are going to use stove or wood fire. Don't take more pots than necessary. Nesting pots which fit inside each other are handiest. Bail handles should lock into upright position. Sigg seems to have put more thought into their design than others. Most outdoor cookpots are made of aluminum; light stainless steel would seem better, but these are hard to find.

• **Pressure Cooker.** If you don't mind the weight and are particular about how your food is cooked, a pressure cooker may be worth considering. Remember that the boiling point of water drops with elevation gain, so that water-boiled foods take longer to cook the higher you go. At 8,000 feet, cooking time is approximately double that at sea level. The pressure cooker cuts cooking time in half and conserves fuel and food values, too. A group might consider taking one. Recreational Equipment of Seattle markets a 4-quart, 2- to 4-man capacity pressure cooker that weighs 3 pounds and is 6-1/2 inches high and 6-1/2 inches in diameter.

• **Pot Gripper** The steel pot gripper with a spring-loaded grip works best.

• **Sierra Cup** A beautifully designed outdoor cup. Made of light stainless steel with a steel wire that circles around the rim of the cup and extends out in a loop to form a hooked handle. The wire helps draw heat off the rim so that you don't burn your lips when drinking. With this cup you don't need anything else to eat or drink from. You can even cook a bite in it. Be sure to get the genuine article. On the inside of the cup scratch a mark to show the height of one measuring cup—about 1/2 inch down from the rim. (3 ounces)

• **Large Water Container** You can add latitude to your trip by taking a large (1 gallon or better) container for water. It gives you the option of camping away from water, and is especially handy if you are cooking. Now that most wilderness areas ask you to camp at least 100 feet from water, carrying such a container becomes an even better idea. No special kind. Any light, plastic, 1-gallon bottle with a handle, such as you find holding supermarket beverages, will do. The thought of it dangling from your pack may offend you, but you could think of it as adding a little of the hobo to your backcountry style. You would, of course, carry it empty and use it only in camp.

There is a ready-made product of 2-1/2-gallon capacity that folds very small when not in use. It consists of a nylon fabric sack which supports within itself a double-layer, sheet-plastic bag with faucet. It is equipped with ties so it can be hung from a branch.

OTHER UTENSILS
• **Pocket Knife** It's probably some ancient feeling that prompts us to take more knife than we need into wilderness. All that's necessary is a good pocket knife (one of the simpler Swiss Army knives) that has one good blade, an awl, a screwdriver for prying and a can opener—or some such combination. The blade should be sharp, good for cooking, cleaning fish and the usual knife chores. A well-made hunting knife is a beautiful and useful thing, but it isn't really necessary.
• **Spoon** Only eating utensil necessary. A tablespoon with a long handle is best for stirring.
• **Spatula** For frying.

- **Scotch Brite** Excellent cleaning pad for pots.
- **Salt and Pepper Shakers** Buy the packaged picnic size or the two-section plastic container for salt on one side, pepper on the other.
- **Grater** A small peeler or grater can be handy.

FOR STORAGE
- **Plastic Bottle** One-quart, wide-mouth, tight-sealing, screw-cap. For mixing powdered milk and fruit drinks, making kefir and soaking dehydrated vegetables while on the move.
- **Hard Plastic or Aluminum Containers** 3 to 4 inches diameter, 2 to 3 inches high. Tight-sealing screw top. For provisions that don't pack well in plastic bags, like butter and honey.
- **Plastic Bags** Lightweight, see-through, strong plastic bags in small, medium and large sizes. Before leaving, repackage what foods you can into these bags. You may repackage in bulk, or into smaller, premeasured units to save measuring in the field. Packaging into bags eliminates corners and makes stuffing into your pack easier. Label bags of hard-to-identify items with a marking pen. Convenient, and yet—when you consider that it takes about a thousand years to biodegrade a plastic bag, it makes you wonder if we shouldn't go back to reusable cloth and rubberized cloth bags, or bags of

70

coated nylon fabric. If you use plastic bags, recycle whenever possible and never leave them behind in wilderness.

GRILL
You can do without by arranging the stones of the fireplace so that pots can rest on them. But a ready-made grill of lightweight stainless-steel tubing, big enough to hold two pots, can be handy.

STOVE
Stoves are of two kinds: the gas-burning stove and the butane-cartridge stove. The gas-burning stove (Svea, Optimus, Primus and others) requires a ritual to light. It's also noisy and somewhat susceptible to malfunction. The smell of gas is unpleasant. There is also the possibility of gas leakage from the stove or fuel container into the pack, contaminating the food. Still, some people swear by them. Gas-burning stoves do burn hotter than butane-cartridge stoves. The Phoebus 625, which burns white gas, is rated to boil 1 quart of water in 4 minutes; the Bluet butane-cartridge stove is rated to boil 1 quart of water in 10 minutes.

The butane-cartridge stove (Bluet, Primus Grasshopper) is a more compact unit and much more convenient than the gas burner. It requires no priming, preheating or pumping; just open the valve and light. It burns fairly quietly and the cartridge eliminates the need for carrying fuel in a separate container. Keep track of cartridge content by scratching time elapsed on the side of the can.

The disadvantages of stoves, either kind, are their weight and bulk and the fact that you can cook only one thing at a time.

MISCELLANY

Listed neither alphabetically, nor in order of importance, nor in any order at all, just as they might end up in your pack, here are miscellaneous items to make or break your trip.

• **Dark Glasses** For snow and desert. At higher elevations sunlight becomes especially intense. On early-season mountain trips, you will be crossing snow. If you must cross an extensive snow field and you don't have dark glasses, looking through a small hole or slit cut into any opaque material will save your eyes. A neutral gray lens gives most natural color vision in bright sunlight. Amber heightens vision in low visibility conditions. Green is restful. Avoid exotic colored lenses.

• **Toilet Paper** Never as much as you think you'll need. To save bulk, unroll off cardboard tube, reroll flat and stow in plastic bag.

• **Aluminum Half-Tube Tent Stake** (8-1/2 inches, 1-1/4 ounces) An excellent digging tool. Makes digging a privy hole easy and is worth carrying just for this purpose. No excuse then for a haphazard job.

• **Mirror** Polished steel. For signaling. For looking at the animal once in a while too.

73

- **Camera** If you are into photography, you will want to take a camera. But don't get hung up taking pictures. No camera can capture the space of wilderness. But then there are always those transporting shots that come close.
- **Binoculars** You don't need them, but if you are willing to carry the weight, they can heighten a moment here and there. A monocular is perhaps more to a backpacker's convenience. Bushnell puts out a model that has two interchangeable lenses, 8 by 24, and 6 by 18, either of which can also be used as a magnifying glass. It weighs just 4 ounces.
- **Kuban-Hitch** For those who want to carry their camera or binoculars at the ready, L. L. Bean offers a cleverly designed elastic harness that holds your equipment at chest height, snugly against your body. Does away with carrying your equipment flopping and swinging from your neck. Has instant release. The pack can be worn right over it. (4-1/2 ounces)
- **Matches** Waterproof stick matches rather than book matches.
- **Insect Repellent** Cutter Insect Repellent Cream is recommended. But whatever kind you use, put it on carefully and then forget it. Don't let insects get you down. They're fellow creatures with a natural right to be where they are, doing the things they're doing. Don't be a mindless killer of bugs.
- **Lip Salve** Necessary.

- **Sun Lotion** Necessary. Don't forget your nose.
- **Flashlight** A small, truly dependable flashlight has yet to be invented. And are flashlights really necessary? They're one of those things you need only if you have one. The compact 3-1/2-ounce Mallory is a popular choice, but no more reliable than average. It is a good idea, when carrying a flashlight stuffed in a pack, to put a piece of tape over the switch so that it doesn't turn on accidentally and drain the battery. Or, reverse the battery when not in use.
- **Rubber Bands** They weigh nothing, take up no space and are very handy. Take different sizes.
- **Toothpicker** To have something stuck in your teeth and nothing to pick it out with is trying. A few toothpicks, or a length of dental floss or fishing line will do.
- **Toothbrush** In wilderness, somehow, brushing with plain old bicarbonate of soda (baking soda) leaves a more natural taste than candy-flavored pastes.

- **Extra Specs** If you're prone to breaking them, take a spare. If you have prescription dark glasses, take them for the spare.
- **Candle** Household candle or the short, thick plumber's candle. Candles are waterproof and useful for starting fires.
- **Sewing Kit** One strong needle, a length of strong thread, safety pins, and some ripstop tape.
- **Watch** If you have the habit, take one. If not, know what time the sun rises and sets, the length of the day.
- **Plastic Bags** A few extra of all sizes. Waterproof, airtight, see-through—a very handy package. Best closed with rubber bands.
- **Soap** Instead of bar soap, liquid soap in a small plastic squeeze bottle with a screw top and a locking squirter. Before you take it, make sure it doesn't leak. All-purpose soap, not detergent.
- **Towel** Is a big towel necessary? At most, a terrycloth face towel or smaller washcloth. Either one of these, with two or three bandannas, should serve all towel needs.
- **Arkansas Whetstone** (1 ounce) For sharpening.
- **Books** A good trail guide can be helpful, or a natural history guide of the area you're traveling through. In wilderness, book-reading seems idle somehow, especially when backpacking.
- **Notebook** If you're a scribbler and don't like to lose thoughts, or you want to keep a log of the trip or do some sketching, take a notebook. A 3-1/2- by 6-inch notebook bound with thread up the long side with tape over the spine is durable and good for carrying in the pocket. A short stub of pencil will hold inside the notebook. Spiral-bound books don't work as well.

- **Music** Jews'-harp? Harmonica?
- **Watercolors** If you're into painting, why not? A watercolor sketch-block packs and carries well.
- **Canteen** It seems like a first-rate canteen has yet to be invented. An ideal canteen would be light, carry well, cap securely, and be of material that won't spring a leak or impart flavor to the water. A quart or 1-1/2-pint size seems right. You would want more capacity where water is scarce. The soft polyethylene canteen with attached plug and screw cap is a light and fairly durable product. Water weighs just over 2 pounds per quart.

- **Instant Knapsack** The kind that tucks into its own zippered pocket. Made of coated waterproof nylon. Shouldn't weigh more than 4 ounces. Opened it should hold about a cubic foot of stuff. Good for day trips from a base camp.
- **Belt Pouch** Worth considering for those who want small items close to hand. Fastens to belt with loops.
- **First-Aid Kit** The point is to do what you do in such a way as not to be hurt. The most common outdoor injuries are said to be cuts, then sprains, strains, bruises and fractures, in order of frequency. Hands and fingers are hurt most often, then feet and toes, then legs. Sharp hand tools cause the most injuries. There is no reason at all to get hurt in wilderness. It's now one of the safer places in the world to be. Alertness and care in all you do, and doing things within an honest measure of your capacities are the best preventatives. But there is always the off-chance of injury, and the first-aid kit is mostly for this. You can get a ready-made kit or make up your own. A somewhat

elaborate kit would include the following. Amounts will be determined by the length of your trip, number in party and your proneness to injury. Average amounts for a party of three.

Adhesive tape, 1 inch by 5 yards

Assortment of Band-Aids, 20

Gauze bandage, 2 inches by 6 yards

Gauze pads (3 inches by 3 inches), 5 packages— 3 to a package

Ace bandage, 1 roll

Moleskin, amount determined by how well your boots fit, 1 package at least

Zinc oxide, 1/2-ounce tube

Antibiotic ointment, 1/2-ounce tube

Salt tablets, 30

Aspirin tablets, 30

Codeine or other heavier-than-aspirin pain pill— consult your doctor here

Antibiotic for major infection—consult doctor

Cutter's Snakebite Kit

Water purification tablets, if you are going where the water isn't fit to drink

The kit can be made even more elaborate with the addition of such items as ammonia inhalants, a space rescue blanket (single sheet of mylar silvered on both sides, 2 ounces), and a splint. There are wire splints and inflatable plastic splints: a plastic tube that can be fitted over the arm or leg as a splint or compression bandage.

Remember your personal or prescription medicines which require regular dosage.

Read up on first aid before you go in.

• **Fishing Gear** Keep it compact. A simple bait-fishing outfit would include: telescoping or sectioned rod, reel, line, leader, size 14 hooks (for salmon eggs), snap swivels, sliding sinkers and salmon eggs. Check the Last Whole Earth Catalog on handline fishing. Check out handy scissor-pliers from Eddie Bauer.

• **Manicure Set** Perhaps a tweezer and file.

• **Calendar** It's possible to lose track of days in wilderness. In your notebook write out a calendar for the days you'll be in and mark them off as they pass.

LAST WORD ON EQUIPMENT

Equipment is the part of the trip that costs the most. The idea of this rather extended chapter has been to give as thorough a knowledge of equipment as possible, so that when you buy, you will know pretty much what to look for. Then you won't buy an inadequate piece of equipment to start with and have to discard it and buy the same item over again in better quality—an expensive way to learn. You can, of course, suffer with inadequate equipment, but what for?

On the other hand, you don't want to become an equipment freak. This is a tendency somewhat encouraged by manufacturers of outdoor equipment who are now onto the merchandising game of a new model each year for many of their items. They also cater to our national fetish for having things as convenient as possible with a proliferation of new backpacking equipment. Some of the products have been truly innovative, while many others have been of questionable value.

The wilderness trip is more than just having the latest equipment. If you did it right, you could even go in with a funky outfit you made yourself and still get the total experience. The idea is to be well enough equipped so as not to take anything away from wilderness except water, some wood (if it's down and abundant) and perhaps some fish to put the country into your flesh. Remember you are just passing through and you are not leaving a trace.

Finally, if you're in a party and not fully equipped, you're going to have to borrow from a friend. But your friend is traveling minimum, and if you borrow, he suffers. It's not right. Have your outfit as complete as you can make it before you go in. Borrow or rent equipment if you can't buy it. Many sporting goods stores rent backpacking equipment.

NEXT TIME
The next time is going to be better if you learn from this time. When you get home and after you're rested, check over your pack. How did your equipment function? What did you miss? What didn't you use? Resolve to go lighter and simpler next time.

FOOD

One mark of our so-called "advanced techno-
logical" society seems to be that we eat too much.
We tend to take things out on eating. We have
diseases caused mainly by overeating. Yet at the
same time, strangely, we have anxieties about not
having enough to eat. Part of this anxiety is believ-
ing that unless we have three square meals a day,
every day, we'll begin to starve, or get sick immediately. Something called "dietary deficiency" is
presented to us as a constant threat to our health
and well-being. You wonder how our species man-
aged to survive to this point without knowing the
minimum daily requirements.

Then to make matters worse, the advanced-tech
society wants its food processed, which thins out
nutrition, requiring more of it to be eaten to make
us feel nourished. So we eat and eat. Every sign
seems to say: Eat. It's no longer a question of
nutrition, it's psychology. We overeat to fill a maw
of insecurity. We eat, grow fat and feel partially
secure. If we take this food style into wilderness,
we're bound to take more than we need.

Much of this state of affairs is reflected in the variety of specially prepared camping foods offered the backpacker. Check the catalog of any store that carries a complete line of dehydrated and freeze-dried dishes. They read like the fantasy of a starving man: Tuna à la Neptune, Chili Con Carne Ranchero, Beef Almondine, Turkey Tetrazzini, Chicken Chop Suey—they've got to be kidding. Then there are packaged menus for breakfast, lunch, dinner, snacks and desserts that go the same way. The whole American food trip freeze-dried. It seems something better could be thought up, something more in keeping with the spirit of wilderness. How long can we go on using a gift of such beauty as fire to cook up freeze-dried Turkey Supreme? Even white flour biscuits, bacon grease and coffee have more the feeling of proper outdoor grub.

With food as with all else in backpacking, the ideal is to take the minimum to get you by without a sense of deprivation or hardship. There's no need for austerity or fanaticism. On the other hand, say that you've gone in bare minimum, and, for one reason or another, you run out of food a day or two from your car. Well, what's wrong with an honest fast, if it comes to that? Our body has great reserves available to it at all times—how strange never to use them. Our capacity to fast is an interesting and valuable thing to know. How long and how far can you go without food? To know this could be considered an outdoor skill.

In this food chapter let's look at every possibility with an open mind, remembering that everyone must work out his own food approach. Only by experimenting will you find what suits you best outback. You have to do it before you know.

FOOD OUTBACK

What we want in backpacking food is nutrition, flavor, ease of preparation and light weight. The food must also keep well.

NUTRITION

We all know the need for a balanced diet. In wilderness this is especially important. Backpacking is energy consuming. We'll do best at it if we fuel our bodies with the most energetic and substantial foods possible. We need a diet that contains proteins, carbohydrates, fats, minerals and vitamins in quantities sufficient to sustain us through a vigorous outdoor day.

Carbohydrates (sugars and starches) give us fast energy. Energy from proteins comes more slowly but lasts longer. Fats have more energy than

both carbohydrates and proteins, but give it off more slowly than either. The amounts we need of these food elements is a question impossible to answer except in the most general terms. It would be good to have some idea of the minimum daily requirements for these elements. But there are too many variables to say, for instance, that 4,500 calories per day is the average need for a body at work. Biochemically there is no average man.

We all have some idea of the amounts and kinds of food we need to function at rest and at work. It's best to rely on this more or less intuitive sense of our individual nutritional needs when planning food for a trip. It doesn't hurt, however, to study up a little on basic nutrition.

For those who like to calculate the numerical values of food, there is a book published by the U.S. Department of Agriculture that gives a run-down on the nutritional value of 2,483 separate items of food—everything from abalone to zwieback. *Composition of Foods*, Agriculture Handbook No. 8, U.S. Department of Agriculture. For sale by the U.S. Government Printing Office, Washington, D.C. 20402. Price, $3.60.

FLAVOR

Clean air and exercise always make food taste better in wilderness, unless you're in the mountains with a touch of altitude sickness. Sometimes, appetite and taste take unexpected and whimsical turns

—foods you'd never think of eating at home become delicious outdoors. In fact, what you normally eat at home and what you eat backpacking may work out to be very different.

When thinking of flavor, however, don't forget nutritional value. Foods with high nutritional value that taste good to you are to be chosen over favorite foods of dubious value.

EASE OF PREPARATION

Whether you enjoy cooking outdoors or not, it's wise to take food that requires minimum preparation. Most of your supply should not require cooking at all; food which takes over 30 minutes to prepare definitely needs a second thought. This is not only for convenience. In most areas open to backpackers, wood is no longer abundant. Even if you're using a stove, you can carry only a limited amount of fuel.

Have a store of food that's versatile: not so much definite breakfast, lunch and supper foods, but foods that can be eaten in any combination and at any meal.

LIGHT WEIGHT

Ideally, we want the most energy and nutrition in the lightest weight and bulk. Water is the main weight factor in food, so look for foods which have been dehydrated to some extent. Concentrated foods like seeds, nuts and grains are excellent—high energy and nutrition in small bulk. Aim for about 1-1/2 pounds of dry food per person per day. However, weight should not override other considerations. If you prefer fresh food to the lightweight freeze-dried, take it along and cut down weight in other things.

PERISHABLE FOODS

If the label says "keep under refrigeration," don't take it on a trip of more than several days. Such things as fresh or cooked meat sealed in plastic seem to keep better if the package is broken open so the contents can breathe. But, of course, things that melt, like butter and soft cheese, should be put into tight-sealing plastic containers. In hot weather, anything perishable should be carried in the center of the pack where it is cool. A natural refrigerator can be made by placing perishables in a large cookpot, covering pot and placing it, well anchored, in a stream or lake.

CORNUCOPIA

The following is a partial list of foods that might be taken into wilderness. Something (hopefully) for every taste.

MECHANICALLY FREEZE-DRIED AND DEHYDRATED

The trend now in outdoor food is toward mechanically dehydrated and freeze-dried food. Dehydrated food is prepared by placing the food in a vacuum chamber and drawing its water out with heat. In freeze-drying, the food is flash frozen at 140°F below zero, then placed in a vacuum chamber where the temperature is very quickly raised to 180° above zero. This causes the frozen water in the food to vaporize without turning to liquid first—that is, to sublimate directly from the solid to the gaseous state. The food is then packaged airtight. This process leaves mineral salts intact, rather than having them carried off by the evaporating juices, as happens when food is dried by heat alone.

The lightness and compactness of food processed in this manner would seem to make it the ideal outdoor food. But is it? The question is, can you submit food to such harsh treatment without devitalizing it? Can you withdraw up to 98 percent of the water from something organic, as happens in freeze-drying, and not have it change into something entirely different? And when you do add water to it, does it reconstitute, or merely soak up water like a sponge?

Freeze-dried foods are notorious for not digesting well. They are said to retain a fair amount of their nutritional value, but what good is this if they won't digest? You get some taste, but do you get any nutrition? Proper digestion requires energetic food. The energy of food is held in the chemical bonds of its molecular structure. When you process a food you break down its structure and de-energize it. It would seem that highly processed food lacks the structure for proper digestion. A lot of freeze-dried passes through undigested.

Freeze-dried foods may be purchased as separate vegetables, fruits and meats and also combined into pre-cooked dishes. The pre-cooked dishes use synthetic food chemicals and are so heavily seasoned that it's hard to taste the actual food. When you do, it's often bland and flat. A monosodium glutamate flash.

• **Fruits and Vegetables** Strawberries, peaches, apricots, apples, banana flakes, prunes, yam flakes, string beans, corn, cabbage flakes, peas, carrot dices, mushrooms, celery flakes, potato dices, onion flakes, tomato flakes, spinach flakes, red and green peppers.

• **Freeze-dried Meats** For use as additives, diced hamburger, chicken, beef, ham and corned beef. Then there are freeze-dried beef steaks, pork chops, meatballs, pork and beef patties. Beef jerky.

- **Powdered Beverages** Orange, grapefruit, pine-apple and tomato drinks; chocolate, strawberry and vanilla shakes; powdered milk; instant coffee, tea and cocoa; Tang, grape and orange; Wyler's fruit-ades; a large selection of powdered soups; bouillon powder or cubes.
- **Desserts** There's also a variety of freeze-dried and dehydrated desserts, mostly instant and non-cooking: puddings, gelatins, cobblers, pies and ice cream. Junket-rennet tablets.
- **Other Protein Sources** Freeze-dried cottage cheese. Freeze-dried and powdered eggs (2 table-spoons powdered egg mixed with 2-1/2 table-spoons water equals 1 fresh egg.). Chunks of dehydrated soybean flour to be used as additives: beef, ham and bacon flavors.

COMPRESSED FOODS

The latest in freeze-dried foods is compressed freeze-dried food. Freeze-drying removes up to 90 percent of the original weight of a food; now, by compressing the freeze-dried food, a 75 percent to 90 percent reduction in size results. This size reduction permits carrying three to five times more in the same space. Compressed foods will rehydrate to almost original size and appearance. They come as separate vegetables and meats or as prepared main course dishes.

There are also compressed precooked meats, such as Wilson's bacon bar and meat bar. The 3-ounce meat bar contains precooked meat equivalent to 1/2 pound of raw meat and 500 calories.

MIXES

Pancake, cornbread, biscuit, gingerbread, applesauce and fruit mixes are packaged and require just the addition of water and some cooking. Try preparing your own mixes. Pan breads and cakes taste good outdoors, if you are willing to go to the extra trouble.

Then there is the Middle Eastern falafil mix of garbanzo bean flour and spices with which a tasty vegiburger can be made. See recipes.

NATURAL FOODS

• **Beans** Most beans, while highly nutritious, are a bother because they require such long cooking. The soybean is a worthwhile exception. It is delicious precooked and nutritionally almost a meal in itself. See recipes.

• **Nuts** Best purchased in bulk at natural food stores. Almonds, brazils, cashews, filberts, macadamias, peanuts, pecans, walnuts, pignolias. (The pignolia has a greater protein content than meat.) Nuts are best eaten raw. If you roast them, do so as little as possible. Nut butters may also be purchased at natural food stores or prepared from scratch.

• **Seeds** Pumpkin, sesame, sunflower, chia. Sesame butter. Seeds are lightweight, tasty, nutritious—they're ideal for snacks. See recipes.

• **Dried Fruits** Dates, apricots, peaches, raisins, figs, currants, pineapple, pears, prunes, apples,

coconut, papayas and nectarines. Sun-dried fruits are best and about the only places that carry them are natural food stores.

• **Grains** Brown rice, barley, millet, buckwheat, cornmeal, rolled oats, wheat, wheat germ, bulgar (parboiled wheat). Some of these make good breakfast cereals—either cooked or dry like granola-type cereals. See recipes.

• **Herbal Teas** Peppermint, mu, sassafras, mint blends, flower blends—the list is endless.

• **Dairy Products** Butter and cheeses. Canned butter keeps well in the field. Kefir, which is like a liquid yogurt, is relatively easy to make in the field, using powdered milk. Some health food stores carry kefir culture in powdered form. Any kind of soured milk tastes good in wilderness.

• **Breads** Pilot bread, biscuits and crackers. The dense compact pumpernickel bread. Oroweat or Golden Gate breads, which come in sealed airtight packages, will stay fresh in the field two weeks easily and probably more. Also, thin Scandinavian wafer breads or Ry-Krisp type crackers.

• **Sweets** Honey, sugar, chocolate, fruit bars, maple sugar brick, Kendel mint cake, high-energy protein bars and quick-energy candies, available at health food stores.

• **Spices** Salt, pepper, herbs. Fresh home-grown herbs taste great outdoors and will perk up freeze-dried and dehydrated foods. A dash of curry powder will do the same. Cinnamon for stewed fruit. What about an all-purpose blend? See recipes.

• **Old Country Foods** Dried fish and shrimp, dried and powdered kelp, miso, teas, soy sauce, salami and other dry sausages, cheeses. Japanese instant soups and noodles. Instant noodles can be found packaged separately and are a versatile item. They require but a minute or two of cooking and can be combined with other foods in a variety of ways. If you are carrying fresh vegetables a fast chow mein can be made. See recipes.

FRESH FOODS

Fresh foods are generally ignored by backpackers because of their weight and perishability. But there is nothing you miss in wilderness so much as the taste of something fresh. It would be good to know wild, edible foods, but failing this, you might think of taking in a few items of fresh food.

• **Fruits and Vegetables** Some oranges or crab-apples tucked away in odd corners of your pack. Small amounts of fresh vegetables are worth their weight for the zest they add to your cooking. Certain vegetables keep very well: carrot, cucumber, green chile pepper, sweet Bermuda onion, to

mention a few. Roots and tubers do well but you must consider their weight and bulk. Of these, Jerusalem artichokes are light and nonbulky. Fresh herbs, even if they wilt. A small piece of ginger and some garlic for sure. A few fresh lemons for salad dressing and for trout should one be caught. Lemon or lime juice that comes in a plastic squeeze bottle works also. Avocados are always tasty outback. Take fairly ripe avocados as green ones don't seem to ripen well in a pack. Pack avocados in cookpot to avoid mashing.

- **Fresh Eggs** A great hit outdoors, however prepared. Carry them in a plastic egg carton (generally of a size to hold just small eggs). Hard-boiled eggs eliminate the breakage problem and keep well, even better if dipped in paraffin to seal the shell.
- **Sprouted Seeds** These can be carried in with little trouble, and they weigh nothing. Alfalfa sprouts are especially delicious outdoors. It's best to start your sprouts before going in. They can be

carried in a clear plastic bag hung on the outside of your pack. Sprouts need air and should be rinsed at least twice a day. To do this, fit the mouth of the plastic bag onto a small embroidery hoop—this gives you an open-mouthed container to put the sprouts in—then cover the mouth of the bag by fixing nylon mosquito netting onto the hoop.

FOOD SUPPLEMENTS

A variety of powdered protein drinks is sold in natural food and health food stores. They come in different flavors and are worth consideration. If you don't mind the taste of brewer's yeast, a hot cup of it can really set you up in the morning. Get the instant-mixing kind. If you are eating mostly processed food, it would be a good idea to take a multivitamin preparation containing the principal vitamins in amounts close to the recommended daily requirement. It would do no harm to take at least one gram of vitamin C a day, especially if you

are prone to colds and infections. The 500 milligram tablets are most convenient. If your stomach goes off kilter outdoors, try taking acidophilus tablets.

EXOTICA

Then there are foods just lately brought to our attention, such as bee pollen and the royal jelly of bees. Bee pollen is an extremely nutritious food containing protein, minerals, vitamins (especially B-complex), free amino acids, and enzymes. It has a flavor unlike that of any other food, like some very concentrated bittersweet, tart bread/candy. You must taste it to believe it. Bee pollen is said to be good for cardiac action and intestinal function. The fact that it's said to increase hemoglobin count makes it an excellent high-altitude food. Buy it in its natural pellet form.

Royal jelly is a glandular substance produced by the worker bee and fed to bee larvae together with honey and pollen. It is rich in nucleic acids. The Chinese make a kind of tonic based on royal jelly. The tonic is liquid and generally comes in a 10 cc glass vial. Taste it on an empty stomach to see what it does for you. A vial of this is a fine way to start an extra-hard wilderness day. If your health food connection can't get it for you, try a Chinese pharmacy.

Someday a dedicated backpacker will go through the whole Chinese pharmacopoeia in search of herbs and medicaments helpful to the outdoor life. Like the legendary ginseng, for instance, which modern research has shown to be an excellent tonic for the central nervous system and a regulator of blood pressure. If you are in the mountains, which is a yin condition, the yang of ginseng will provide a nice balance.

FOOD STORES

It's impossible to do the food shopping for a trip in one store. You'll have to shop around.

The most complete selection of dehydrated and freeze-dried foods will be found in outdoor and sporting goods stores, along with other outdoor food items like canned butter (Darigold).

The supermarkets have surprisingly little you'd want to take into wilderness. Most of their food is highly processed and fixed with synthetic food chemicals.

Natural food stores are excellent for dried fruits, nuts, seeds, grains, flours, cheeses, oils and nut butters. Some natural food stores carry organic freeze-dried vegetables.

Health food stores carry food supplementation items: vitamins, high-protein powdered drinks and quick-energy candies.

It's possible to find many dehydrated and concentrated foods in stores that cater to different ethnic and national groups. Japanese and Chinese stores carry dried fish, shrimp, seaweed and mushrooms prepared in a variety of ways, as well as concentrated foods like miso (soybean paste). Japanese stores have packaged instant soups and instant noodle dishes. European delicatessens are good for dry sausages and cheese. When buying dry sausages like salami, buy the chub unsliced.

HOW TO FIGURE FOOD AMOUNTS

Make a calendar of the days you'll be out. Count the number of breakfasts, lunches and suppers you'll be eating. Add food for trail snacks, plus food you'll eat car-traveling to and from your destination. Say you will need seven suppers. Figure out the menu for each one, noting approximate amounts and weights. Calculate breakfasts, lunches and snacks in the same way. Add up the amounts and weights of each different food. This is your shopping list.

We usually tend to take more food than we'll need. Figure you'll eat less than you think. Go over your list several times and eliminate or cut down where you can. About 1-1/2 pounds per day of fresh or dry food seems right, give or take according to size of appetite.

SEVEN-DAY MENU
(Party of Three)

See recipe section for preparation of dishes given here.

BREAKFAST
An extra long or hard hike (called a "grunt" among hikers) is sometimes better done on an empty stomach; it feels light and vital to do work on your reserve strength. It can be like coming into your second wind. Or, if you don't feel so spare and austere, perhaps a light breakfast of some nuts and dried fruit. Or maybe just an orange, or a cup of plain hot water, or a protein drink, or a shot of ginseng-royal jelly tonic.

But not to be parochial on the side of the natural and simple, here follow breakfasts in more or less the traditional mode. Remember, breakfast can be anything that appeals to you that morning.

On cold, wet days, eat hearty at breakfast to keep up body heat.

1. Stewed Fruit. Oatmeal. Milk. Hot drink.
2. Fresh orange. Scrambled Eggs with Herbs. Toast. Milk. Hot drink.
3. Stewed Fruit. Pumpernickel French Toast. Milk. Hot drink.
4. Fresh orange. Blaise's Sierra Cereal. Milk. Hot drink.
5. Fresh orange. Dried fruits and nuts. Peter Flash Bar. Milk. Hot drink.
6. Dried fruit. Cheese and Sprouts Omelette. Toast. Milk. Hot drink.
7. Pancakes topped with Stewed Fruit. Milk. Hot drink.

LUNCH

Lunch is pretty much the same each day. No cooking. Make your own combinations from foods such as salami, cheese, sesame butter, peanut butter, bread, crackers, nuts, seeds, dried fruit, alfalfa sprouts, roasted soybeans, fruit drinks or powdered tomato juice. Lunch is also a good time for any taste flash you might have brought along, like a small can of sardines.

Lunch need not be more than a snack—too large a lunch can make you feel logy. You could eliminate lunch altogether by snacking lightly through the day. This makes dietary sense in that your body expends less energy for hiking. Sometimes a cooked lunch is nice for a change, like on a layover day when you aren't hiking.

SUPPER

Supper is the meal you look forward to, unless you're too bushed to think of eating at the end of a hard hiking day. Supper is generally your most

elaborate meal. It is when you practice your *haute cuisine*, if you have it. Try to make your supper fairly substantial—it is the last meal of the day and your body will be able to digest it thoroughly while you rest. Suppers can be less elaborate and varied than those on this menu. You could, for instance, eat the same basic stew every night, touching it up differently each time, or do the same with a basic sautéed vegetable-protein dish. You must work out your own outdoor food style.

1. Bouillon. Blue Spruce Soufflé. Bread or Janet Brown Crackers. Salad. Dessert. Hot drink.
2. Bouillon. Far Country Chow Mein. Cheese. Salad. Dessert. Hot drink.
3. Bouillon. Mountain Stew. Sierra Cup Cornbread. Salad. Dessert. Hot drink.
4. Bouillon. Cheese Pot. Salad. Dessert. Hot drink.
5. Bouillon. Paternoster Egg Foo Yung. Roasted Soybeans. Salad. Dessert. Hot drink.
6. Bouillon. Brown Rice Pot. Salad. Dessert. Hot drink.
7. Bouillon. Fresh Trout. Herbed vegetables. Trout Bone Garbage Soup. Janet Brown Crackers. Salad. Dessert. Hot drink.

RECIPES TO BE PREPARED AT HOME

PREROASTED GRAIN

Preroasting or parching grains at home saves cooking time in the field. Roast the grain in an iron skillet on the stove over medium heat. Keep stirring. Cook till the grain just changes color and begins to smell roasted.

PARBOILED RICE AND GRAIN

Any grain can be parboiled (partially boiled ahead of time) to save cooking time outback. For parboiling use 1-1/2 parts water to 1 part grain or rice, except for millet which requires 2 parts water to 1 part millet. Bring to a boil, then simmer till water is gone and the grains are separate. A mush won't do. Spread out parboiled grain on a cookie sheet and dry in a low-heat oven. Don't overdry, just enough to pack well. In the field, cook 15 minutes with 1-1/2 cups water to 1 cup parboiled grain.

ROASTED SOYBEANS

Soak beans overnight. Drain and spread on lightly oiled cookie sheet. Roast at 350° about 1-1/2 hours, or till golden brown. It's important to turn them often. While hot, pour on soy sauce, lightly covering all the beans, and stir. Can be eaten as is or added to stews.

ROASTED PUMPKIN AND SUNFLOWER SEEDS

In separate pans, roast raw seeds over low heat in a little butter or oil, stirring frequently. Roast pumpkin seeds till they puff out slightly, sunflower seeds till they just lose their raw taste. Combine roasted seeds in a bowl. While they are hot, gradually add soy sauce to taste, stirring until the soy sauce is absorbed. Good trail food.

BASIC HERB BLEND

Combine 3 parts dried parsley with 1 part each dried marjoram, basil and thyme. Tarragon and/or chervil may also be added.

BLAISE'S SIERRA CEREAL

In a large bowl, mix together:

4-1/2 cups (1 pound) rolled oats
1-1/2 cups (1/2 pound) pumpkin seeds, chopped
   to size of oats
2 cups (1/2 pound) sunflower seeds
1 cup (4 ounces) shredded coconut
1/4 cup (2 ounces) sesame seeds, ground in blender
1/4 cup (2 ounces) raw wheat germ

Blend together and add:

1/2 cup warm water
3/4 cup honey
1/4 cup crude sesame oil
1 heaping teaspoon salt
1 heaping teaspoon lecithin

Mix well, spread out on cookie sheet and bake at 275°, stirring often, till golden brown.

Now add:

2 cups (3/4 pound) currants
1/2 cup (4 ounces) banana flakes

Stir often as mixture cools. Eat as is, or with milk.

TIM'S TRAIL FOOD ✓

2 cups (1-1/2 pounds) chopped almonds
2 cups (1-1/4 pounds) chopped walnuts
2 cups (2/3 pound) chopped dried apricots
1 cup (1/3 pound) raisins
1 cup (1/3 pound) chopped dried pineapple
1 cup (1/2 pound) chopped pignolia nuts
1 cup (1/4 pound) sunflower seeds
1 handful (1/4 pound) diced carob bar

Combine all ingredients together and package in a plastic bag for quick-energy snacks or dessert.

KATIE MOM HONEY-NUT GRANOLA

What is required for this recipe is any homemade or storebought trail munch that includes ingredients somewhat along the following lines: Brazil nuts, pecans, walnuts, almonds, cashews, roasted soybeans, currants, raisins, peanuts, sunflower seeds, sesame seeds, chia seeds, cut up dried fruit. The nuts and seeds should be raw. Chop large nuts to about the size of an almond.

1-1/4 pounds trail munch
3 to 5 cups (about 1 pound) rolled oats
1-1/2 cups honey (approximately)

Mix trail munch and oats in a large mixing bowl (6-quart size). Oil your hands. Add honey gradually, tossing to just coat the ingredients, no more. Spread out a batch onto a large cookie sheet, but not too thickly. Roast at approximately 400° for 30 minutes or until golden brown. Watch carefully, turn over at least once. Don't let raisins burn! Continue baking in batches till done.

PETER FLASH BAR

Lots of calories. For those times when you want energy in a rush, for instance, before, during, or after a long, hard grunt. Some of it while you're in your bag of a cold morning or evening will help warm you. Also a good dessert.

1 cup honey
1 cup peanut butter
1 cup unsweetened carob powder
1 cup walnuts (or any other nut)
1/2 cup sesame seeds
1/2 cup chopped dried apricots
1/2 cup raisins (Monukka)
1/4 cup shredded coconut

Heat honey till it's runny. Mix in peanut butter, carob powder and walnuts first; then follow with the rest of ingredients. Compact into bars or balls and wrap in plastic.

OATCAKE

3 cups (about 3/4 pound) rolled oats
1/2 teaspoon salt
1 teaspoon cinnamon
1 tablespoon oil
1 teaspoon vanilla
1 cup boiling water

Mix dry ingredients with oil and vanilla. Stir boiling water into mixture and let sit for 15 minutes. This will make a stiff batter. Roll batter to 1/4-inch thickness and cut into cakes. Brown both sides of cakes in unoiled iron skillet. Then dry the cakes out in a 200° oven for a half hour. This cake will keep well in the field.

THE JANET BROWN CRACKER

Everybody likes grain. Here is a cracker that could serve as the entire grain portion of your backcountry diet. It is both bread and cracker. It is good with butter, cheese, or with any nut butter and honey. It can be broken up and put into soup for thickening. It can be eaten by itself. A really fine grain hit outdoors.

8 cups (2 pounds) whole wheat flour
2 cups (2/3 pound) cornmeal
1 cup (1/4 pound) rye flour
1 cup (1/4 pound) raw wheat germ
3/4 cup (1/4 pound) sesame seeds
3/4 cup (1/4 pound) ground sunflower seeds
1 teaspoon salt
2 cups vegetable oil
2 cups water
1/4 cup soy sauce (tamari)
honey to taste (not more than 1/2 cup), or
    molasses or malt syrup for a stronger flavor

Hand mixing does best in this recipe. Mix dry stuff. Add oil and work in till you have a dough like for pie crust. Mix water, soy sauce and honey in a blender; add to oiled mixture and work in with

114

hands. You want a dough that's on the firm side, and not sticky. Don't knead. Make balls and roll out on a well-floured board. (Cornmeal would be good for dusting board; for one thing, it adds color to the surface of the cracker.) Roll dough out to about 1/4-inch thickness or less. Cut into 3-inch squares. Put on a greased cookie sheet and bake about 15 minutes at 350°. They will crisp as they cool, so don't overbake thinking to crisp them in the oven.

For a more elaborate cracker, some or all of the following ingredients could be added, or used as substitutions.

2 tablespoons (1/2 ounce) chia seeds
2 tablespoons (1/2 ounce) caraway seeds
2 tablespoons (1/2 ounce) poppy seeds
buckwheat flour and/or soy flour and/or soy milk
    powder may be added or substituted for any of
    the other flours
pinch of cayenne, or any other seasoning you
    think will work
2 to 3 teaspoons brewer's yeast
grated Parmesan cheese, to taste but not more
    than 1 cup (1/4 pound)

For an even more interesting cracker, take half the oil, 1 cup, and in a frying pan fry-cook the following vegetables, finely chopped.

1 large onion
3 to 4 cloves garlic
1 bunch parsley

Cook till flavors pass into the oil. Set aside to cool, then blend this mixture with water-soy sauce-sweetener liquid and add to other ingredients.

RECIPES TO BE PREPARED IN THE FIELD

Field cooking over a wood fire has a magic quality that can't be approximated by cooking with a gas or butane stove. The experience is more total, what with the beauty of an open fire. A pine wood fire, say, with its resiny fragrance and direct, radiant heat. It's oddly fulfilling to sit by a fire at twilight with a pot of slumgullion at a bubbling simmer before you. It is so ancient.

But wood gets more and more scarce in wilderness and you can carry in only a limited supply of stove fuel. If we must cook in wilderness, a fast cookery would seem to be the order of the day. Rather than boiled dinners, which take time—you must, for instance, first bring water to a rolling boil before anything else happens—perhaps we should go more to the faster cookery of light, quick frying, or sautéing. Lightly fried foods have a clean, fresh taste outdoors that's very satisfying. Boiled dinners may be more ample and filling, but if after your light omelette or chow mein you still feel hungry, you can always munch goodies out of your store. After all, isn't it just a spot of warmth and flavor we want from cooked foods outdoors?

COOKING DEHYDRATED
AND FREEZE DRIEDS

When you buy, know whether you're buying dehydrated or freeze-dried. They cook differently. Most dehydrated food needs a lot of presoaking, freeze-dried relatively little. If you're using dehydrated vegetables for supper, start soaking them in your plastic bottle several hours earlier while on the move. Dehydrated foods want a lot of cooking, too. They are best used in long-cooking stews and should be avoided in quickly cooked dishes.

PUMPERNICKEL FRENCH TOAST

1 package (2-1/2 ounces) powdered
   scrambled egg mix
raw wheat germ (optional)
6 slices pumpernickel bread
butter

Combine egg mix with water according to package instructions and add wheat germ to taste. Dip bread slices in mix and fry in buttered pan. Eat with cinnamon and honey.

SCRAMBLED EGGS WITH HERBS

1 package (3 ounces) freeze-dried eggs
1 package (1-1/4 ounces) freeze-dried ham bits
1 teaspoon Basic Herb Blend
butter

Combine eggs and ham and pour 1 cup boiling water over them. Let stand for 5 minutes. Add herbs and scramble in butter.

CHEESE AND SPROUTS OMELETTE

1 package (2-1/2 ounces) powdered scrambled
    egg mix
raw wheat germ (optional)
1 small garlic clove, thinly sliced
butter
sliced cheese
alfalfa sprouts

Combine egg mix with water according to package instructions. Add wheat germ to taste and garlic. Pour into hot buttered pan. When the underside appears almost cooked, lay sliced cheese down the center and fold egg over. Cook till the cheese begins to melt. Garnish with alfalfa sprouts.

STEWED FRUIT

Soak dried fruits overnight in pot. Apricots, peaches, prunes, apples, raisins, pears, or some such combination. Cook next morning with several slices of orange. Don't overcook. Add honey if you want it sweeter. Cinnamon?

TOASTED CHEESE SANDWICH

Place slices of pumpernickel bread in hot buttered frying pan. (Pan-fried bread is good by itself and easier to prepare than toast.) Lightly fry and turn over. While other side fries, put on slices of cheese and fresh onions. Continue cooking until cheese begins to melt. Garnish with alfalfa sprouts. Thinly sliced salami or crumbled bacon bar can also be added.

MOUNTAIN STEW

1 package (4 ounces) Maggi oxtail soup mix
1 package (2 ounces) freeze-dried meatballs
1 handful each dehydrated peas and carrots
several slices fresh onion, chopped
2 handfuls roasted soybeans
raw wheat germ (optional)

Prepare soup mix according to package instructions
and bring to a boil. Add meatballs, vegetables and
onion. Simmer until meatballs are cooked. Add
soybeans and wheat germ if desired; cook until
beans are hot. Add more water if stew starts to dry
out and stir to keep stew from sticking.

BROWN RICE POT

3 cups water
2 cups parboiled brown rice
1 handful chopped pignolia nuts
1 handful pumpkin seeds
1 handful sunflower seeds
2 handfuls chopped dried apricots
1 handful dehydrated peas
1 handful fresh thin carrot slices
1 garlic clove, chopped
1 palmful chopped onion
wheat germ to taste (optional)
cheese slices

Bring water to a boil and add other ingredients
except cheese. Stir to mix well and cook, covered,
over low heat for 20 minutes. Just before serving,
lay cheese slices on top and allow to melt.

CHEESE POT

1 package (4 ounces) Maggi cream of chicken
   soup mix
4 cups water
1 package (3/4 ounce) freeze-dried green beans
3 handfuls parboiled brown rice
1/3 pound cheese, cut into 1/2-inch chunks
3 slices toasted bread

Combine soup mix and water and bring to a boil.
Add beans and cook until beans are tender. Then
add rice and cheese to mixture and cook another
five minutes, until cheese is heated but not melted.
Serve over toast.

CHOP SUEY

1 handful (1 ounce) dehydrated or freeze-dried
   mushrooms
sesame oil
1 small garlic clove, thinly sliced
2 slices onion
2 handfuls dehydrated shrimp
1 carrot, whittled into thin strips
alfalfa sprouts
soy sauce

Reconstitute dried mushrooms. Heat oil in frying
pan with garlic. Add onion, shrimp, mushrooms
and carrot and cook quickly until vegetables are
tender but still crunchy, stirring as you cook. At
the last minute add alfalfa sprouts. Crumbled
bacon bar or freeze-dried meatballs may be substi-
tuted for the shrimp. Flavor with soy sauce.

PATERNOSTER EGG FOO YUNG

You worked up into a basin past a string of lakes. Paternoster lakes. You set up camp beside a lake at treeline. Chinese water and mountain landscape. A quick-cooking egg dish.

1 package (3 ounces) freeze-dried eggs
raw wheat germ, to taste
1 handful thin carrot slices
1 garlic clove, sliced thin
2 thin slices onion
crumbled cheese
1 handful alfalfa sprouts

Reconstitute egg according to package instructions. Combine with all other ingredients. Heat butter in pan and spoon egg mixture into pan to form patties. Fry lightly on both sides. Season with soy sauce.

FAR COUNTRY CHOW MEIN

Chow mein has to be one of the most basic dishes ever invented. Noodles and vegetables. Meat optional. A fast-cooking dish. First, prepare instant noodles and set aside, or, once cooked, you may want to pan-fry them. Fresh vegetables do best, of course. Cut up vegetables—perhaps, garlic, onion, green chili pepper, carrot. Some sliced fresh ginger. Sauté vegetables in oil in your largest pot. Have pot hot so that when you throw in vegetables and dash small amount of water over them there is crackling and steaming. Alternately cover and stir-fry wok style. Add just enough water to steam-fry vegetables 5 minutes or so and still leave enough liquid for sauce. Thicken liquid slightly with arrowroot, cornstarch or flour. (Always prepare thickener separately, with enough water to make runny paste, then pour into pot. Thickener put directly into hot liquid tends to lump.) Season lightly. Just before taking vegetables off fire, mix in noodles and stir thoroughly.

Serve immediately with soy sauce at hand and a little hot mustard if you are carrying it, the powdered kind mixed with a little water. Freeze-dried meatballs are a fine meat addition; rehydrate and cook with the vegetables.

BLUE SPRUCE SOUFFLÉ

This is a quick-cooking dish. It needs a fair bed of coals. The puffed egg effect works best with fresh eggs. First, cut and sauté whatever fresh vegetables you're carrying. Carrots, green chili pepper, onion and garlic would be a good combination. Sauté in the pot you'll be using. Season to taste with salt, pepper and Herb Blend. With fresh eggs, separate yolk from white. In a separate pot, whip white till stiff, using a pronged twig as you would a whisk. Beat yolk and mix in with sautéed vegetables; then fold in white. Cover pot and bury in coals to at least a third of the way up side of pot. Put coals on top of cover also. Cooking time will depend on thickness of pot and amount of coals. In any case, it should cook within 15 minutes; check after about 10 minutes. Don't overcook. As the soufflé firms up, sliced cheese may be laid on top to melt. A good brown crust will form around side and on bottom. Garnish with alfalfa sprouts. Powdered egg may be used but the soufflé won't rise as much as with fresh eggs.

MOOSE VEGIBURGER

Going up beaten path up Avalanche Canyon, Tetons, met moose in bog. That evening at Lake Taminah where it outlets into Shoshoko Falls, a friend named Moose cooked this vegiburger.

Falafil mix is generally a natural food store item. The idea of the falafil vegiburger is this: Cut up and sauté whatever fresh vegetables you are carrying, say, garlic, onion, carrot, green chili pepper and alfalfa sprouts. In a separate container mix 2 tablespoons powdered egg with 2-1/2 tablespoons water (or use a beaten fresh egg); add sautéed vegetables. To this mixture gradually add falafil mix until you have batter thick enough to form patties. Keep patties thin. Fry patties in oil or butter about 5 minutes each side. Eat with alfalfa sprouts and soy sauce.

MOUNTAIN TROUT

Melt butter in frying pan over steady medium heat. Lay in trout and cook about 5 minutes on each side for a trout 1 inch thick. The rule is that fish should be cooked 10 minutes per every 1 inch of thickness measured at thickest part of fish lying flat. Salt while cooking. Trout won't stick to the pan if you fry it covered. When they start to curl, cut and flatten them.

TROUT BONE GARBAGE SOUP

Perhaps you are lucky enough to have the Golden Trout of the high country for supper. Fresh caught. Golden sided with reddish strip down middle and parr marks superimposed. Bright red detail down middle of whitish belly. Light salmon-colored flesh. Delicate flavor. Now, there are the bones, fins and head, the skin and some flesh, lying in the pan in a butter and fish oil sauce left from the cooking. Is it garbage, or the base for a soup?

This soup will clean the pan also. Add water to pan and set soup on stove or fire to boil, then simmer. Slice fresh ginger thin and throw into soup. Garlic and onion, too. Wild onion if you have come across any. If you had lemon slices with the fish, throw them into soup also, rind and all. Throw in any other garbage that might add flavor. Season to taste with salt, pepper and soy sauce. A pinch of cayenne. Simmer till the flavor of all the ingredients has passed into soup. You will be the judge of that. Drink soup through teeth to sieve out bones and garbage. A truly bracing soup outdoors.

SIERRA CUP CORNBREAD

The cookpot can be a Dutch oven of sorts—within, a cornbread baked in a Sierra cup. Any bread or cake could be baked in this same manner. You have a good bed of coals and you don't want to waste them. You don't have chestnuts or marshmallows, nor anything to barbecue. You do happen to have some cornmeal. The recipe specifies 1 egg. If you are using powdered egg, the equivalence formula is: 2 tablespoons powdered egg mixed with 2-1/2 tablespoons of water equals 1 fresh egg.

1/2 cup cornmeal
1 rounded teaspoon baking powder
1/4 teaspoon salt, or a mite less
1 egg
1 tablespoon oil
1/4 cup milk, or enough to make a stiff batter

Mix dry ingredients. Beat egg and oil together. Pour milk into dry mixture while stirring, until a stiff batter forms. Add egg-oil mixture and work into batter. Place batter in a buttered Sierra cup. In bottom of pot place about 3 stones of a size to raise cup 2 inches or so off bottom of pot. Place cup on stones and cover pot. Pile coals around the pot and on the cover. Be sure there is a good bed of coals under the pot. Should bake in 20 to 30 minutes. Check toward last with toothpick. If toothpick comes out with dough clinging to it, cook longer. Dry toothpick indicates done. Delicious with butter and honey.

SALAD

Even if it's just a bite, fresh salad is a worthy taste outdoors. Say you're carrying fresh carrot, onion, garlic, alfalfa sprouts, Jerusalem artichoke, avocado and cucumber, the English or European cucumber if you can find it. Into a pot, put thinly sliced cucumber, onion, Jerusalem artichoke and garlic. Whittled or grated carrot. Finely chopped fresh ginger. Alfalfa sprouts. Spooned out pieces of avocado. Mix and season with salt, pepper and/or Herb Blend. For a change, dress with soy sauce and sesame oil. Lemon juice could be added to this. This may seem like rather an elaborate salad but it really isn't.

DESSERTS

Organic sun-dried dates and Calimyrna figs are like the world's best confection. If you want to bother with puddings and suchlike, there's a variety of freeze-dried desserts on the market. They will add to your overall food preparation time, however, as well as your pot-washing chores. The Peter Flash Bar makes a good dessert.

THE NONCOOK TRIP

Fires are beautiful, but they want attention and wood. There is not much pleasure cooking on a dinky gas or butane stove. When cooking in the field you may feel a certain urgency that is not entirely pleasant—especially when cooking for more than one. Are you out there to slave over a hot stove? Then there's the matter of washing pots, and the weight of pots and stoves. A noncook trip is worth considering.

There are many varieties of food that don't require cooking. Cheese, bread, seeds, nuts, dried fruits, precooked meat bars, jerky, dry sausages, sweets, sprouts, other fresh vegetables and fruits, granola-type cereals, an oatcake perhaps, beverages, high-protein drinks and other supplemental foods.

You could go far and high on a store of raw almonds and Brazils, a jar of raw honey (or a brick of maple sugar), a bag of bee pollen, a small chunk of ginseng, some vials of royal jelly, a bag of dates, a bag of dried apricots, some fresh fruits and vegetables, together with whatever supplementals you might need or want, like a hip flask of Remy Martin.

PEMMICAN

Then there is the idea of a pemmican of your own fashioning. Pemmican is the idea of carrying a single item of food that is compact, digestible and nutritious, that would taste good to us at all times of day, day after day. It must not require cooking on the trail. The pemmican of the American Indian was jerky (mainly protein) and rendered fat. The early American outdoorsman made a pemmican of jerky, fat, raisins and sugar, which added some carbohydrate and minerals. If we could make a pemmican of high caloric content that contained protein, fat, carbohydrate, minerals and vitamins, we might have something more to our idea of a fully nutritious food.

Here, let's broaden the definition of pemmican to mean any compact, nutritious, tasty, uncooked or precooked foodstuff that carries well and keeps for a long time—say for at least a month without spoiling or getting rancid. It may or may not contain meat and animal fat. Most important, it must serve as a staple food in place of the collection of separate and various foods traditionally packed in.

A light, relatively nonfatty, meatless, uncooked pemmican might include some of the following.

• **Seeds** Sunflower, pumpkin, chia. High caloric content, both saturated and unsaturated fats, rich in both protein and minerals, some vitamins. Best raw.

• **Nuts** Pignolia, almond. Much like seeds nutritionally. Best raw.

• **Dried Fruits** Pitted dates, apricots, raisins or currants. Dates are an excellent carbohydrate

source, better in fact than most grains. Dates are a fine all-round food of high caloric content. In addition to carbohydrate, they have some protein and are rich in minerals. There are many varieties of dates; choose the one that suits your taste—the Empress is a fine variety. Dried apricots are extremely high in vitamin A. Sun-dried fruits are the best.

To these basic ingredients might be added things like raw wheat germ, wheat germ oil, a little salt, some vitamin C powder (just enough to give the pemmican a slight tart, clean aftertaste—if you can find powdered fruit vitamin C, like acerola, all the better), some kind of high-protein powder, bittersweet chocolate chips, etc. You can either mix all these ingredients as they are, or put the whole thing through a hand grinder set at coarse.

The ingredients and the amounts must be determined according to your own taste. When you compress the stuff to pack it, the stickiness of the dried fruit will bind it nicely. Around 3/4 pound a day of the stuff, more or less, should provide all the calories and nutrition you need.

This pemmican can also be made into a pemmican biscuit. Simply add flour, milk and egg to the pemmican mixture in quantity sufficient to make a dry, stiff biscuit batter. Mix well, roll out and cut into flat rectangular biscuits for efficient packing. Then bake on a cookie sheet at 300° for 20 to 30 minutes on each side, or until you have a dry biscuit. Check often to test. Here again, you may use the ingredients as they are, or coarsely grind some or all of them. With the addition of carob powder, powdered chocolate or something like Ovaltine, you will have a sweeter biscuit.

A meat pemmican can be made by adding shredded jerky, crumbled-up bacon bar or ground-up dry salami to the seeds, nuts, dried fruits, etc. Lecithin might be added to this mixture to help the body assimilate the animal fat.

You may want to take both the saltier meat pemmican and the sweeter pemmican biscuit. In addition to your pemmican, you might carry a few items like powdered milk and some fresh fruits and vegetables that keep well like orange, apple, cucumber and carrot, tucked away in your pack here and there.

Imagine not feeling obliged to cook. It would be a different trip. More leisurely. Of course, a noncook trip doesn't preclude a fire altogether, or heating a Sierra cup of water for a hot drink now and then.

GETTING THE TRIP TOGETHER

You are planning to be out a week. The date and the place have been set. Perhaps a mid-season trip to mountains. An easy walking trip. You'll do a loop. Five days walking and two days layover. The layover days will give the trip flexibility.

Say it's July, and that you'll be at altitudes between 9,000 and 12,000 feet. You expect the temperature to range between 40° and 85°F. You know that mornings before sunup and evenings after sundown it's going to be chilly, and that you can expect thundershowers midday. For the rest, it will be warm to hot, and hotter when you do the day's hike. You expect mosquitoes.

You are a party of three—seems wise not to go out alone the first time. Companions who share an understanding. Going out with others is always an exercise in alertness and manners. Character quirks tend to become accented outback. Go with people you trust.

You are in good shape and you are outfitted. You have gotten together and planned a menu. You are taking less rather than more. The food has been bought and repackaged into plastic bags whenever possible.

Equipment has been checked and repaired where needed. You have seen to the condition of your boots especially, and Sno-Sealed them. You have checked your clothes and mended where needed. Your toenails are carefully trimmed for walking. The tooth that's been troubling you has been fixed.

You have the maps you'll need and you've studied them. You know the route and the approximate location of each of your camps along the way. You have noted where ranger stations are along your route. You have your camping permit or plan to pick it up at a station in the field. You have left a complete itinerary of your trip, from home to wilderness and home again, in the hands of a reliable friend. This also has the approximate date you'll be at each camp. Then you've checked the weather forecast for the week you'll be in.

You've replaced that worn tire, tuned the motor and you're confident your car will get you there and back. You've packed along extra food to munch on the way and maybe a clean set of clothes for when you come out.

You have avoided a last-minute rush.

MASTER CHECK LIST

This list doesn't include every item mentioned thus far in the book. It is a selection, made as broad as possible, yet with some idea of consistency. Its attention to weights is to point up the fact that you must have some idea of how much each item you are taking weighs, and just as important, an idea of its bulk. When figuring out the stuff that you'll take, consider the size of your pack, and the weight-bulk factor of each item you will put into it. It takes some doing to get the feel of it.

The food list is based on the seven-day menu described in the previous chapter. The assortment of foods may seem odd, but we are trying to be perfectly eclectic. We are dealing in possibilities. It is hard to imagine anyone taking just this list of foods. Check it against your own ideas of back-country food, and come up with the food trip to suit just you.

Brand names mentioned are recommended. We have aimed for a pack weight for each person of about 30 pounds.

CLOTHES

2 pairs underpants, 4 ounces
well-worn T-shirt, 4 ounces
cotton crew-neck, rib-knit,
    long-sleeve shirt (Skyr), 10 ounces
1 pair pants (Can't-Bust-Em), 1 pound, 8 ounces
heavy wool shirt (L.L. Bean North Woods Shirt),
    1 pound, 10 ounces
shell parka (North Face), 1 pound, 4 ounces
poncho (Sierra Designs), 1 pound

wool-knit watch cap, 3 ounces
3 bandannas, 3 ounces
3 pairs socks (Wick-Dri), 10 ounces
1 pair boots (Pivetta 5), 4 pounds
1 pair slippers, 8 ounces

This is approximately 12 pounds of clothes. About half of this weight will be worn while hiking, leaving 6 pounds for the pack.

PERSONAL MISCELLANY

dark glasses or clip-on, 1/2 ounce
insect repellant (Cutter), 1 ounce
sun lotion, 1-1/2 ounces
lip salve, 1/2 ounce
toothbrush, 1/2 ounce
baking soda or tooth powder, 2 ounces
washcloth, 2 ounces
notebook and pencil stub, 2-1/2 ounces
Sierra cup, 3 ounces
spoon, 1 ounce
canteen (1-1/2-pint soft polyethylene with
        attached cap), 3 ounces
instant knapsack, 4 ounces
nail file, 1/2 ounce
comb, 1/2 ounce
compass, 1-1/2 ounces

This adds up to a weight of approximately 1 pound, 6 ounces.

EQUIPMENT

pack and frame (Sierra Designs), 3 pounds,
    12 ounces
sleeping bag (lightweight), 2 pounds, 12 ounces
foam pad (North Face, 20" x 36"), 17 ounces
tarp tent (10' x 10', coated ripstop), 1 for
    party of three, 2 pounds
nylon cord, 100 feet, 6 ounces

This basic equipment comes to about 10 pounds.

COOKING UTENSILS

2 cookpots (nesting, 2-1/2-pint and 3-1/2-pint
    pots), 1 pound, 4 ounces
pot gripper, 3-1/4 ounces
salt and pepper shaker, 1-1/4 ounces
Scotch Brite
tin foil, 10" square piece
potato peeler, 1/2 ounce
spatula, 2-1/2 ounces
2 plastic wide-mouth quart bottles, 8 ounces
stove (Bluet), 1 pound
2 butane cartridges, 1 pound, 6 ounces
stove windscreen, 4 ounces

This is approximately 5 pounds, 5 ounces, or approximately 1 pound, 12 ounces per person.

COMMUNITY MISCELLANY

toilet paper (1 roll), 7 ounces
aluminum half-tube tent stake, 1-1/4 ounces
mirror, 1-1/2 ounces
matches, 1 ounce
flashlight (Mallory), 3-1/2 ounces

rubber bands, 1 ounce
candle, 4 ounces
sewing kit, 1 ounce
plastic bags, 2 ounces
soap (liquid in plastic squeeze bottle), 7 ounces
knife, 3-1/2 ounces
whetstone, 1 ounce
camping permit
fishing license
first-aid kit, 5 ounces
fishing gear (including bottle salmon eggs),
        25 ounces
scissor-pliers, 1/2 ounce
maps
guidebooks

This totals approximately 4 pounds, or 1 pound,
5 ounces per person.

FOOD

butter (canned or fresh), 1-1/2 pounds
cheese, 2 pounds
fresh eggs (6 small), 10 ounces
salami, 12 ounces
Wilson's bacon bar (3 bars), 9 ounces
fresh oranges (7 small), 2 pounds
fresh English cucumber, 1 pound
fresh carrots (7 small), 1 pound
fresh Bermuda onion (1 large), 1 pound
fresh Jerusalem artichokes, 1/2 pound

avocados (7 small), 1-3/4 pounds
fresh alfalfa sprouts, 1/2 pound
fresh garlic, 1/4 pound
fresh green chile pepper, 1/2 pound
fresh ginger, 1 ounce
Oroweat pumpernickel bread (1 package), 1 pound
Janet Brown Crackers, 1-1/2 pounds
Blaise's Sierra Cereal, 1-1/2 pounds
Tim's Trail Food, 1-1/2 pounds
cornmeal (1/2 cup), 2-1/2 ounces
rolled oats (1-1/2 cups), 5 ounces
parboiled brown rice (1-1/2 cups raw rice),
    12 ounces
raw wheat germ, 8 ounces
brewer's yeast, 8 ounces
falafil mix, 12 ounces
pancake mix (1 cup), 6 ounces
instant noodles (1 package), 6 ounces
Peter Flash Bar or other high-energy candy,
    12 ounces
pignolia nuts (1 cup), 8 ounces
almonds (2/3 cup), 8 ounces
roasted salted pumpkin seeds (1-1/2 cups), 8 ounces
roasted salted sunflower seeds (2 cups), 8 ounces
roasted salted soybeans, 1 pound
dates (2 cups, pitted), 1 pound
dried apricots (3 cups), 8 ounces
raisins (1-1/2 cups), 8 ounces
dried figs (1-1/2 cups), 8 ounces
freeze-dried eggs (2 packages), 6 ounces
powdered scrambled egg mix (2 packages), 5 ounces
freeze-dried meatballs (1 package), 2 ounces
dried Japanese shrimp (1 package), 1 ounce
freeze-dried ham bits (1 package), 1-1/4 ounces
freeze-dried peas (1 package), 2 ounces

freeze-dried mushrooms, 1 ounce
freeze-dried green beans (1 package), 3/4 ounce
freeze-dried carrots (1 package), 1 ounce
Maggi oxtail soup mix (1 package), 4 ounces
Maggi cream of chicken soup mix (1 package),
    4 ounces
Maggi bouillon cubes (22 cubes), 3 ounces
Wyler's fruit drinks (5 1-quart packages), 15 ounces
herbal tea (Lhasa Karnak green mountain tea)
    or instant coffee, 4 ounces
Milkman instant dry milk (7 1-quart packages),
    1 pound, 10 ounces
honey, 1 pound
vegetable oil (1/2 cup), 4 ounces
soy sauce (1/2 cup), 4 ounces
salt, pepper, spices and herbs, 1 ounce
baking powder, 1 rounded teaspoon
bee pollen, 8 ounces
vitamins, 1-1/2 ounces
plastic bags (for repackaging the above), 2 ounces

This is approximately 36 pounds of food. Divided
into three, this gives you approximately 12 pounds
per person to carry and eat.

TOTAL PACK WEIGHT

clothes—6 pounds
personal miscellany—1 pound, 6 ounces
equipment—10 pounds
cooking utensils—1 pound, 12 ounces
community miscellany—1 pound, 5 ounces
food—12 pounds

This adds up to a total pack weight of approximately 32-1/2 pounds. Not bad.

THE WALK IN

It is eight hours to where you're going. You've decided to leave home before dawn to be there in time to walk to your first camp while it's light. It's still and quiet as you drive away from home. The world is asleep. You are awake. It's a kind of solitude. The quiet pleasure of driving down empty streets early mornings. And you drive. Long freeway that carries you nonstop to your destination. Three companions hurtling along, high on the deep excitement of change. As you go higher the air becomes clearer and cleaner. Then turn off freeway onto the road that takes you straight into the mountains. You park your car at 9,000 feet.

ROADHEAD, TRAILHEAD AND IN

You brought your provisions in a box. Now spread your tarp or poncho on the ground, lay everything out and look at it. Do you still think you need all you brought? As you stow things into your pack eliminate again. You'll find it's mostly food you set aside. Now you have everything you'll be needing for a week. Lock your car. Take key. Put on sun lotion, insect repellant and lip salve if needed.

Lace boots so they feel supportive. Long drink of water. On with pack. The load should feel compact The shoulder harness should hold the pack snug against your back with no lateral sway. Hunch up your shoulders to lift the pack, then fasten the waist-belt and cinch it up fairly tight. The load should now be riding on your hips. Fuss with your pack and get it feeling right before you start. As you go along, keep adjusting the shoulder harness and waist-belt till you know how the pack feels best on you. Some people think their pack is wrong, when actually, they aren't wearing it right. The 30 pounds should feel like a part of yourself—or almost so.

At the trailhead, sign the register if there is one. Sign all trail registers you come to. Now you are ready to walk in. Start off slowly. You've agreed no one will set a pace and lead. Each one will find his own pace at first without the group becoming too separated. If one of your party feels uncertain, stick by him. How does your pack feel now? If it doesn't feel right, adjust it again. If your hips get tired, loosen the waist-belt and shift the load to your shoulders for a while. Don't ever suffer a discomfort you can fix.

BLISTERS

How do your boots feel? If they pinch or rub painfully anywhere, stop and put moleskin on the spot *before* a blister forms. Don't neglect your feet, they're your only mode of transportation. If you find you've developed a blister, attend to it pronto. If it is just a tender redness or a small blister that hasn't ballooned, simply cover it with moleskin. If it has ballooned, pop its underside with a cauterized needle and drain it, leaving the loose skin intact. Then cover the spot with moleskin. Leave the moleskin on till after your hiking day is over. When you remove the moleskin, the loose skin will probably fall away. If the loose skin doesn't come off, but feels like it should, trim it off gently. Let the wound air. Next morning put on more moleskin. Some people recommend putting moleskin on a drained blister and leaving it on till the blister heals. Either way, take care of blisters. Sore feet can spoil a trip. If you know your boots to be tight at certain points, put moleskin on for protection before you start hiking.

TRUCKIN'

But say your boots are well broken in, you don't have blisters, and you're walking easy. You're carrying your pack well. Keep its weight directly over your feet. Keep your forward lean as small as possible. Keep your step toed-in, low and flatfooted for good balance and weight distribution. If the terrain gets rough, shorten your step. Step around rather than over obstacles. Don't take long or high jumps and don't run downhill with your pack on. Remember you're 30 pounds heavier. Take it easy for the first few days. Your body is acclimatizing to the altitude.

MOUNTAIN SICKNESS

The symptoms are weakness, dizziness, headache, nausea, vomiting and insomnia—singly or in combination. The body is reacting to a decrease in oxygen supply. As barometric pressure goes down with altitude, oxygen tension goes down too, making it more difficult for the body to supply itself with oxygen. The body is also stressed by exertion, exposure to wind, dryness, cold and heat, higher intensity of light and gravitational changes. These factors combine to make you feel done in.

Almost everyone feels the altitude to some degree. The only thing to do is take it easy and acclimatize. Cut down on your eating. Big meals divert blood from general circulation to the digestive process and make you feel worse. Listen to your body—when it's mountain sick, it won't want to eat. Do what it tells you and eat lightly at scattered intervals through the day. Skip lunch if you're hiking while sick.

Don't forget to drink plenty of liquids. You are breathing more at higher altitudes in order to take in extra oxygen. But exhaled breath contains moisture. The more you breathe—especially in dry mountain air—the larger the water loss through expiration. As a rule, you underestimate your water loss in the mountains. Dry air and wind evaporate sweat quickly, and so you tend to believe you aren't sweating much. But you are, and unless you replace this water, you will dehydrate.

Remember, too, you're losing salt with sweat. If you're sweating heavily and feeling mildly sick from dehydration, take a salt tablet and water. Extra salt and water are especially important during the first few days of the trip when the body is

going through its heaviest acclimatization changes. Don't worry, your body will adapt. It is putting out more red corpuscles for extra hemoglobin to carry oxygen through the body.

You can help your body acclimatize by guarding against overexertion and overexposure. Weather can change fast in the mountains. Adjust your clothes to changing weather conditions.

Some people suffer from insomnia during the early acclimatization period. Don't be concerned. Some people never sleep well at higher elevations. Even if you don't sleep, your body can receive solid recuperative rest through the night. Don't toss and turn and worry about not sleeping. Lie as still as possible. Watch the Milky Way make its grand sweep across the sky.

One other thing you can do about mountain sickness is to get yourself into good physical shape before you go in. Do training to develop the respiratory and cardio-vascular systems.

KEEP ON TRUCKIN'

So, inevitably, you have a touch of the sickness, but you aren't letting it faze you. You know it's part of a trip into the mountains. It's a beautiful walk through a small glacial valley with one small lake after another. Moderate forest cover of lodgepole and whitebark pine. You've found your own stride—you're not captured by someone else's. Sometimes your companions are in sight, and sometimes not. Why stay bunched up? You lay back. You put on a little steam. There is level. There is up, and some down. The walk has a pleasing rhythm.

You're not letting yourself get mesmerized by the trail so that on coming to, you find you've traveled far, not knowing how long it took or how you got to where you are. Following a trail can do that. You've been keeping track of trail direction changes. You've been backsighting—you get some beautiful views doing this. You've been consulting the map and know the landmarks around. The terrain is sharply defined and it's been easy to match it up with the map.

The trail follows along one side of a stream, then crosses it by means of a felled tree. When crossing a stream unfasten the waist-belt of your pack. Then, if by chance you fall into the stream, it is easier to work out of the pack. Don't be afraid of getting your feet wet. It's foolish to fall simply because you don't want to get your feet wet. Your boots will dry. A walking stick or staff will give you more stability fording.

In the mountains streams run fast and deep during the spring thaw. And a stream will swell through the day where there is snow-melt. Mornings, before the day's heat has begun to melt the snow, streams run lower. Don't cross water unless it can be done safely.

Be aware if you are in a canyon, arroyo or gorge, along a stream, wet or dry, that's known to flash flood in storm season. Never set up camp in such a situation.

You're heading for the pass that will get you up into the high country. The trail to the pass runs by a small cirque with lake. You mean to camp there. Acclimatize that night and the next day, if necessary.

UPHILL

The trail takes a sharp upturn and begins to switch-back. You begin to climb out of the valley. There is a way of walking uphill with least effort. As always, try to keep the weight of your body and pack directly over your feet. Walk flat-footed, even upslope. Continue to keep the step low, and go around rather than over obstacles. Small steps and a slow, steady pace work best ascending. When the climb begins to get steep, shift into the "rest step," which is simply locking the knee of your downhill leg at the end of each step and briefly resting your weight on it. This gives you a little rest with each step. When you make the turn at the end of each traverse, step off in the new direction with your uphill foot. If the trail gets really steep, use a toed-out step or try side-stepping.

DOWNHILL

You're using different leg muscles going downhill. A long descent can be more punishing than a climb. It may be easier on your wind, but it's harder on your muscles. The temptation is to rush downhill. Best to take it easy. Have your boots laced tight so your toes don't hit up front. Keep your back straight. Keep your knees bent to take up shock. Keep your weight over your feet and step flat-footed. Coming down on your heel will jar your spine. Try not to walk heavy-footed. If you pound downhill you'll feel it in the legs next day and especially the day after that.

BREAKS

Some people recommend regular breaks like ten minutes every hour. Others break when they feel like it. Don't stop too soon, but don't wait till you're exhausted. Your break might consist of just loosening your waist-belt and resting your pack on top of a rock. Or you might remove it completely along with your socks and boots. It's good to air the feet now and then. Wick-Dri socks turned inside out dry fast on a hot rock in the sun. Prop up your feet if they're sore. You want the right spot for your break, but don't be so finicky about it that you find yourself walking on and on. By the side of a creek or rill is nice.

A break is a good time to talk over plans. Snack. Repair gear. Readjust pack. Aim for a fairly long lunch break. Whether short or long, remember the overall rhythm of your day's march and keep to it. Start off again before you stiffen up.

TRAILS

What is more ancient to us than a trail? We do trails innately. Ants make trails. The pleasure of walking a trail is like the pleasure of sitting by a fire. Both make you understand you've done them before, other times. Like a turn in a trail that opens out a remembrance deep inside your head.

Main trails in wilderness and primitive areas of national parks and forests are generally well maintained and clearly signed. When a trail passes through forest, trees are blazed at regular intervals along the way. A blaze mark is usually a rectangular spot cut through the bark to the wood at about eye level. You'll know one when you see it. Don't blaze trees yourself—it confuses matters and spoils trees.

Then there are ducked trails. A duck is a cairn —a heap of stones piled atop each other as only

a human hand can do. Ducked trails are most often found over rock-bound, treeless terrain. The ducks are placed at principal points along the way. These trails are quite often obscure and sometimes peter out altogether. If you are going to use one, especially cross-country, do it tentatively. Have an idea of the terrain and direction you want to follow independent of what the ducks might say. Some ducked trails, however, are beautifully precise and clear, with just the right moves to get you exactly where you want to go.

Again, resist the temptation to place ducks and blaze trees yourself. If you want to mark a spot or indicate a direction, think of a more temporary way of doing it. A sign that only you will know.

Knapsack trails are mostly ducked trails. These are trails through rugged terrain that you'd hesitate to travel over with a heavy pack.

TRAILS ARE PUBLIC
When you meet other people on the trail, whether you're walking level, uphill or downhill, step aside and give them the right of way. Don't give a recital of what lies ahead. If they ask for information, tell them what you know as accurately as possible. Have a pleasant word—you're of the same faith.

Don't come up behind another party and dog their heels. Space out. Either pass them, or stop, and let them get ahead. Give way yourself to a party coming up fast from behind you. If you meet stock on the trail, let them pass. Stand quietly where the animals can see you, preferably on the uphill side of the trail. Never spook an animal.

TRAIL CARE

Do what you can to preserve and maintain trails. Don't cut corners on switchbacks. This breaks down the trail and starts erosion. It can also dislodge rocks and set them rolling—a danger to people below. Besides, you walk more steadily by keeping on the trail. Don't litter with candy wrappers and the like. For safety, don't smoke on the trail; wait for a break or when you set up camp. Field strip cigarette butts.

Don't tamper with trail signs. Read all posted notices. If you use trailside shelters and huts, leave them spruce for the next party. Restore wood supply if you took from it.

CROSS-COUNTRY

When you venture into country not served by a trail, you are going cross-country. From a main trail you often see country back further in you'd like to explore. Or you've heard of a basin, lake, gorge, canyon, waterfall, glacier, peak or other place of interest and beauty that you want to see. Perhaps there's a lake or stream with good fishing. Maybe there's another trail you want to get to on the other side of a divide. Then again, you just might want to get off by yourself for a while. If there are no trails, you cross-country.

Cross-country is usually more difficult than trail-walking. Following a trail is like being led by the hand; in cross-country you're more on your own. It requires some preparation and judgment. It wants a cautious approach.

Say you've heard of a beautiful basin no one ever goes to, five miles off the trail. You decide to hike there, bivouac overnight, and come back to the trail next day. You will take only the gear you need, and cache the rest. A good way to do this is to detach the pack from the frame. Put everything you won't need into the pack, and hang it from a tree off the ground and out of the reach of animals. If there are no trees, close pack tight and leave in an out-of-the-way shady spot, maybe with rocks piled on it. (If you ever come across someone else's cache, leave it alone.) If you have an instant knapsack, put in the stuff you're taking and lash it to your frame, together with your sleeping bag and the few other items you'll need. If you don't have a knapsack, put your stuff in the foot of your sleeping bag, wrap the bag around it and lash it to the frame. In any case, go light.

Study your topo map. Find the best route. Look for a high spot nearby from which you can survey your route. Get your directions straight. Estimate the time it will take you to get there;

figure two to three miles per hour level walking, and perhaps two miles per hour or less for rugged or uphill. Always take the easiest, safest route, even if it isn't the most direct. Be alert. Backsight along the way.

If you come across a stretch of talus (boulders), try to hop along the tops of them, rather than climbing up, down and around. Nothing straightens your head faster than boulder-hopping. Keep your eyes several boulders ahead and move steadily and smoothly from boulder to boulder. Occasionally you will have to stop and climb around or over. Rest now and then. Be careful.

If you must climb scree (smaller, gravelly rock), be patient. Climb toed-out or side-step up. Coming down scree is easy.

If you see from below that you'll have to cross snow, try to do it early in the morning while the snow is hard. If it's a long stretch of snow with sun on it, wear your dark glasses. When traversing a snow slope, kick-step along. Avoid steep snow banks. Snow melts faster around the edges of rocks and boulders: Step lightly around them. When descending a snow slope, you might try to glissade (slide down on your feet), but only if you're perfectly confident of your ability. Make a diagonal run, rather than straight down and see that there's an outrun below in case you lose control.

Avoid crossing ice unless you have crampons (metal spikes attached to boots) or an ice ax. The 4-point instep crampons are all you need. If you must cross ice, do so with extreme care, even if it's on the seat of your pants, or on all fours.

Doing cross-country adds variety to a trip. It's good to get free of the trail now and then. Eventually you may want to make most or all of your trip cross-country. But don't attempt it until you are very sure of yourself outback.

LOST, HURT OR SICK

It's harder to get lost than you might think. But on the off chance that you do, sit down and relax. Don't panic. Don't start dashing off in different directions. Think back along the way you came. Study your map. Recall the general direction you took from camp. If there were shifts in direction, try to remember where they occurred, and about how long you walked each way. Recall landmarks. If there's a high spot nearby, climb to it for a view back. Then calmly reconnoiter. If you still can't find your way, stop, gather wood for a fire and prepare for night. You'll be missed. You'll be found. You have reserves aplenty to fall back on.

To avoid getting lost, review noncompass and nonmap methods of orientation before you go in. Know the direction of prevailing winds. Know that a shadow at noon points north. Note that moss grows on the north side of trees and that the tips of evergreens generally point east. Find direction by the fixed North Star, or if by other stars, remember the earth rotates 15 degrees per hour. And there are numerous other ingenious methods.

DISTRESS SIGNALS

Any signal repeated three times is a signal for distress. Mirror signals will transmit 10 miles on a clear day and from the air can be seen at even greater distances. Sound signals are less reliable, they carry best at twilight and at dawn.

Of all distress signals, fire is probably most effective. Build your fire on a high, clear spot—a bright one at night, a smoky one in daylight. If fuel is plentiful, three fires in a triangle is the signal for distress.

UNUSUAL WEATHER

Generally it's good advice not to travel in storms. Caught by rain, crouch under your poncho. If it looks like it's going to storm, pick a spot and set up a tarp shelter. Gather wood if it's available. Batten down the windward side of the shelter. Hole in and wait out the storm. If you're cold, get into your sleeping bag; sometimes it's the best place to be even in the daytime. Stay warm and dry and enjoy the experience. Storms can have an awesome beauty.

If it looks like the storm is going to last, and you're on a schedule, gird up your spirits and walk out. Late spring, summer and autumn storms, whether rain or snow, are usually fast-passing affairs.

In a storm where lightning is striking right around you, crouch low with only your feet touching ground—your rubber soles will give you insulation. Try not to be the tallest thing around. In the mountains, get off peaks and ridges—look for a flat piece of ground rather than stopping on a steep slope where current flows fastest. If you're carry-

ing a lot of metal, put it away from you. Don't take shelter under ledges, in low, shallow caves, under a lone tree, or near the base or edge of a cliff. You would be safe in a forest, or crouched low in a boulder field. Best of all, have some sense of the weather, and get out of an unsafe area before the storm hits.

Being able to read the weather is an important outdoor skill. Knowing cloud types and what they mean is especially handy in weather prediction. Some knowledge in this direction is a must. Weather is a fairly regular phenomenon, though it can be extremely variable at the same time. A storm, for example, goes through regular stages, but each storm is different. It is a pleasure to be aware enough of a storm to feel the warm front at its center pass over, followed by the cold front sweeping in with towering cumulonimbus and showers and rainbows.

On early- and late-season trips into the mountains snow is a definite possibility. If it starts to come down and has the feel of a storm behind it, then stop whatever you're doing and set up tarp or tent shelter. If possible find a spot protected from wind. Hole in and wait out the storm. Don't move in heavy snow and especially in "white-out" conditions. Early- and late-season snow storms are generally light and fast passing. When the storm passes, you will be able to move through crystal clarity of white world around and intense blue sky above.

HYPOTHERMIA

When you read of a death from "exposure" in wilderness, you may be fairly sure it was caused by hypothermia. Hypothermia results from a lowering of the temperature of the body's inner core. The strategy of the body under cold stress is to care for the vital organs of the inner core first. In a situation of sustained cold-wet-wind the body will draw heat from the body surface and extremities to help keep the inner core temperature at around 98.6°F. However, if there is continued heat loss at the body surface and extremities, the inner core temperature will also begin to drop. This is the onset of hypothermia.

We are comfortably warm when our inner core temperature is around 98.6° and our body surface temperature around 90° to 94°. Our body can keep the inner core at 98.6° even with body surface temperature at around 50° to 75°, but this is an extreme situation, and unless immediate measures are taken to warm up, inner core temperature will begin to drop. Below the critical inner

core temperature of 95°, the body can no longer produce enough heat by itself to recover its normal temperature. At this point, unless outside aid is given, the inner core temperature will continue to drop, and within a few hours, at an inner core temperature of around 78°, death will occur.

Hypothermia is mostly a cold weather threat but can happen during the summer at temperatures well above freezing. In cases of hypothermia, the following conditions are usually present in combination. Cold; it need not be extreme. Wet. Rain, fog, snow-melt, immersion, or even a soaking perspiration. Wind. Wind greatly increases the chilling effect of cold and wet. The wind chill factor. The last condition for hypothermia is the likely victim —a person, generally, who is exhausted and unprepared to take protective measures against sustained cold-wet-wind exposure. Inadequately clothed, lacking emergency gear, ignorant of the symptoms of and treatment for hypothermia. Without knowledge of how to prevent it. Bad news.

In summer, hypothermia most often strikes a person in a state of exhaustion who has suffered a thorough wetting, and chilling exposure to wind. The wind need not be that strong, nor the air temperature that low. A temperature of 40°F and a wind of 25 mph gives a wind chill factor in the "very cold" range, just below "bitterly cold." But thoroughly wet clothing can literally "wick" heat

out of the body, and if a chill wind is blowing, or if the person isn't generating extra heat by strong exertion and intake of calories, this wicking action can withdraw heat faster than the body can produce it. This condition in combination with the body's normal heat loss through radiation, conduction, convection, evaporation and respiration, sets the stage for hypothermia.

The first signs of hypothermia are fatigue, intense shivering, lack of coordination, and difficulty in speaking. Advanced symptoms include decrease in shivering, followed by muscular rigidity causing erratic or jerky movements, exposed skin turning blue or puffy, loss of contact with surroundings, amnesia, irrationality, stupor, and finally unconsciousness. But hypothermia need not be fatal.

If ever you detect these symptoms in yourself or in others, immediate steps should be taken to restore normal body temperature. First, prevent further heat loss. Then somehow add heat to rewarm body. Find shelter from the wind to cut down on the wind chill factor. Remove wet clothes and put on dry. Get into dry sleeping bag. Or if not feeling too bad, be active to generate heat, do isometric exercises. Drink warm beverages and eat high-calorie foods. In advanced cases, placing victim in cold sleeping bag isn't going to help. A thoroughly chilled body can't generate heat by itself. In such a case, someone will need to warm the victim with body-to-body contact inside the sleeping bag.

How to prevent hypothermia. To start, be in good physical shape. Avoid exhaustion. Know your reaction to cold-wet-wind conditions in the field and dress and prepare accordingly. Try to avoid getting wet to the skin and chilled. If you do get wet and chilled, don't remain so any longer than you have to. Carry gear against wetness. Poncho, rain chaps, tarp, waterproof matches. In a wet situation, wear a wool shirt with a thick nap for its insulating properties even when wet. Eat plenty on cold, wet windy days—hypothermia weather. Sweets convert most quickly to heat-energy. Remember, if you are cold enough to be shivering hard, you need warmth right away. It's a good signal, don't ignore it.

WILD AND POISONOUS ANIMALS?

It is now well understood in the animal kingdom that man is the most dangerous predator. Since other animals are conscious, intelligent beings like ourselves, they know to keep out of our way given a chance. The only animal besides ourselves who will attack without provocation is the dog whom we've made our creature and trained to express our hostilities.

A rabid animal will sometimes attack and bite without provocation, but this happens rarely. In case it does happen, get to a doctor as soon as possible. An untreated rabies infection is almost certainly fatal. Rabies is a disease of warmblooded animals. Bats are believed to be the commonest carriers and transmitters of this disease.

If you're in bear country, avoid them, especially bears who have become scavengers, dependent on man for food. They're usually found around heavily used camp areas. The bear is only interested in your food so secure it out of reach. In bear country hang all your food up in a tree at night, at least 8 feet off the ground and 4 feet out on a small branch. Don't fight with a bear over food; if the bear has possession of the food, let him keep it. Don't stash food in your sleeping bag at night, bear may smell it and hurt you to get it.

It isn't sound ecological practice to feed animals in the wild.

Then there are poisonous snakes. In the United States there are four types: the rattlesnake, found from low desert to elevations of 7,000 feet and more; the coral snake, found in Arizona and the southeastern area; the moccasin and copperhead, mostly found in the southern states.

Snakes are shy, retiring creatures and will not attack unless provoked or surprised. If you know you're in snake country, take care. Watch where you step. Snakes are sensitive to excessive cold and heat. They hibernate in winter, are out daytimes in spring and autumn and in summer generally go out most during the cool of night.

Rattlesnakes will be found where there is food, water and protection—around waterholes, brush and rock piles. They can strike for a distance about one-third to one-half their total length. But they are not aggressive, and will either retreat or remain quiet and hidden if confronted by danger.

There are two generally accepted treatments for poisonous snakebites, cryotherapy and the cut-and-suck method. The aim of cryotherapy is to immobilize the venom around the bitten spot with cold applications so that the body will absorb the venom slowly enough to neutralize it. This method requires ice or some chemical refrigerant. It isn't a very practical method in the field. The cut-and-suck method works by removing venom from the wound by suction. To be effective, the cuts must be made right after the bite and suction applied for an hour or more. For this method, the Cutter snakebite kit is a complete, compact unit and comes with full instructions.

YOUR HEAD

Backpacking into wilderness is a change, and a vivid change at that. It is a nearly total separation from the normal context of your life. The supportive context. The context within which you know who you are. This is my home. This is my family. This is my job. This is the newspaper I read. These are the things I like and dislike. Suddenly you are not home but in the middle of wilderness. The first reaction is generally one of exhilaration, even euphoria. If this is your first trip, you may also feel some uncertainty, since you don't know what to expect. Then there's that heavy pack and that rough walking. It's no joke. It's strenuous. It can be toilsome and irritating.

Should you have taken this trail? Does your friend and guide—say this is your first trip—know what he's doing? You're beginning to feel the altitude. Your head feels like your skull is too small. Isn't the pace a little fast? There must be an easier trail. The heel of one foot is starting to get sore and you realize that you haven't broken in your boots enough. Stop. A blister already. The trail begins to ascend. Are you really expected to climb that wall? Your pack seems to be getting heavier. You feel like a beast of burden. And it's hot besides. The mosquitoes gather to you like cows to a feeding trough. You begin to yearn for the familiar context of who you know yourself to be. What are you doing out here anyhow?

This negative chain of thought might be avoided if you were to start out with a different attitude. Perhaps the trip could be thought of as a pilgrimage. Like the pilgrimage to the Virgin of Guadalupe where the pilgrims make their way on their knees, or by one full-length prostration after another. Like the pilgrimage of Harding and Caldwell up the Wall of the Early Morning Light in Yosemite. Or like the pilgrimage of Lama Govinda to Kailasa. Well, is wilderness a shrine? And is backpacking a form of devotion?

As you descend a trail and look at the faces of the people coming up, you get the feeling that you are all involved in some mystery or vaster allegory, in which you are all devotees of a space. A space not even outside, perhaps. What you might be doing is a pilgrimage to a more authentic outback inside yourself. But is there an inside and an outside? And you thought you were just backpacking?

Don't let yourself get bogged down in a negative space. When you're doing a tough stretch, you need to boost your body with a certain psychic drive. Do your mantra, if you have a mantra. Take a rosary and say it as you walk. If you have a koan, work on it. Isn't walking a form of meditation?

Say you're climbing a pass and find it rough going. You're thinking of how far you've come and of the thousand feet you still have to go. Take it a step at a time. As a psychic booster, you might think of each step as bringing you one step closer to the time and place of your death. Not in a morbid sense, but in the sense that your life is a journey from one place to another place, and that this wilderness trip is a short segment of that journey, a thing you have to do, a place you have to come to in order to reach the next place. You can't hold back. You've got to go on. If you weren't supposed to be in wilderness, you wouldn't be there. It is a step-by-step revelation of your fate. Let each step be whole, conscious and clear. Keep your head wide open. You get to the top of the pass, or top of the mountain—so where are you?

Here is that cirque with lake. You made it. Now to find your spot and set out your camp.

CAMP

You have followed up the outlet stream of the lake. A slight trail through alpine willow. As you come to the point where the lake spills over to start the stream you get an eye-level view of the lake's surface. Then you scramble over the lip of the basin and there's the lake in full surrounded by peaks and ridges. The intense blue of a biologically poor lake. Blue like the sky, but deeper from the depth of the water. A wind with a cold edge sweeps wave patterns over it. The water laps gently against the shore. Red mountain heather. Treeline. Mostly rock. Scattered whitebark pine. Now find your campsite.

CAMPSITE

What you want of a campsite will depend upon varying conditions, but essentially there are a few things you look for. A level spot for your bed—

sheltered if there is weather. Access to water. Firewood, if you're using it. It should be off the trail
and out of sight and earshot of other camps. National Parks and Forests now ask that you camp at
least 100 feet from water and trails. You may want
your camp to catch the morning sun, especially if
it's a layover or base camp. If you're fishing you
want to be close to the fish. Above all, the spot
must please you.

On a well-traveled trail you'll generally find
that someone has camped before you at almost
every likely campsite—which isn't surprising since
everyone looks for the same things in a campsite,
more or less. Don't choose a spot that looks over-
used, with ground cover worn down by stock or
too much camping. Let that spot rest and renew
itself.

Choose a sandy spot, bare ground, rock or
duff. (Never build a fire directly on duff or humus;
scrape down to dirt or rock in a wide circle around
the fire.) Find a spot that will take the pressure of
your camp without showing it. You want to be
able to camp and then leave with no trace that

you've been there. As more people go into wilderness, it is imperative that we develop this outdoor style of the ultralight camp and camping without leaving a trace.

In choosing your campsite, go easy on nature. Don't cut trees, dead or alive, for any reason. Don't build elaborate rock structures, windbreaks, big fireplaces and the like. Don't disturb soil with holes and trenches. Avoid meadows for a campsite; they break down easily. Don't dig into the turf of meadows for any reason. Besides, they're quite often wet and being open, bottom land, they tend to dew over heavily mornings and evenings.

It tends to be colder and wetter right next to water. It's warmer among trees and beside large boulders. They soak up heat during the day and give it off at night, as does bare ground. Remember, at night cold air flows down valley, close to the ground. Look for a site that shelters you from it. If you like to watch stars, camp in the open. Try to avoid camping on fragile vegetation like the creeping Douglas phlox with its tiny delicate flower. We've agreed, wilderness is a shrine.

SETTING UP CAMP

You want an overnight camp. The wind has stiffened a little so you decide to set out your camp lee side a huge boulder. It is up from the lake in a small stand of pines. Others seem to have camped on the same spot, but it's still neat. There is a small fireplace made of three flat rocks about four feet out from the boulder. Don't build fires against big rocks and boulders; it blackens them. For warmth it is more efficient for you to sit between the fire and the backstop rock. Sensing no rain or heavy dew, you dispense with shelter. Start your fire and boil water for your end-of-hiking-day hot drink.

• **Your Bed** While the water heats, find your sleeping spot. Say you want to sleep somewhat apart from camp and be alone. You know to take a little trouble finding your bed. Try to find a naturally level spot. Don't dig or level. Avoid sloping ground, but if you must sleep on a slope, feet downhill is best. Don't get yourself into a side-roll position. Some care finding the right spot may prove the difference between a restful sleep and a fitful night. Finally you find a level area just large enough for your sleeping bag, protected on three sides by rock and dwarfed whitebark pine, sheared off flat on top by wind. The ground is fine granitic sand. You test the spot, lying down on it. It's perfect, even to the red flowered penstemon at your head.

Clear off sharp stuff from sand bed. Spread out your poncho for ground cloth, then your foam pad. Take out your sleeping bag, shake it and lay it out so it will loft out before bedtime. Fold the sides of the poncho over the bag if it feels like evening will dew.

• **Water** It's come to pass that wilderness waters are being polluted at an alarming rate. It seems apparent we should do no washing or rinsing of any kind directly in streams and lakes. Fetch water and wash everything far back from stream and lake—at least 100 feet. Be sure that dirty water doesn't drain back into streams or lakes. Use soap, not detergent. Bathe out of cookpots.

One of the deep pleasures of wilderness is being able to drink of all the waters you come across. It's of utmost importance that the purity of wilderness water be preserved.

• **Firewood** In well-traveled treeline country, wood is being burned faster than it grows. This is also true around campsites and along most well-traveled trails, even through forests. It has become necessary to use wood sparingly or, in some cases, not at all. The big roaring campfire is out. A small fire or no fire at all. The only kind of wood to be used in wilderness now is down wood, wood lying on the ground. Don't break or cut snag wood off standing trees, live or dead. It destroys the beauty of them. Leave saw and hatchet at home. If there's wood at all, with a little patience, enough can generally be found for a small fire. Use wood like a precious gift.

CAMP KITCHEN

Keep it simple. Set up your stove or fireplace. If you're using wood, build a safe fireplace on a spot sheltered from wind. As always, the fire bed and surrounding area should be cleared of burnable matter down to dirt or rock. Don't build fire on exposed tree roots. If you are in well-traveled country, use an old fireplace, rather than building a new one yourself. If the old fireplace doesn't suit you, rebuild it on the same spot using the same rocks. A flat rock is a handy worktable. Set up your grill or rocks so that your pots sit level and secure. Set out your pots and utensils. Have a pot of water close by for dipping. Put out all the food you'll be using. Before you start cooking, think out the sequence of steps involved. Then go through them with a certain rhythm.

Gather wood—small twigs to thumb-sized and larger sticks. You can make a substantial fire with just twigs and sticks. Have all the wood you'll be needing close to hand and piled according to size.

The fastest and most reliable way to start a fire is with a candle. Fire the kindling with candle, and as soon as kindling catches, draw out candle and snuff it. Done in a matter of seconds. Get a

174

steady blaze going by feeding in thumb-sized sticks. Then add a few larger sticks to build up a bed of coals. When what you're cooking begins a rolling boil, let the fire die to a simmering heat. Hold it there till you finish your boil cooking. The fire should now be right for frying. Frying is best done over the steady even heat of a good bed of coals with some licks of flame.

Your fire should be just getting low as you finish cooking. Build it up again if you want more hot water for hot drinks and dishwashing.

Clean up after meals as soon as possible—it's easier that way. In a party, the cook shouldn't have to wash dishes and pots. If you aren't cooking, pitch in where you can.

At night pack food away securely so small animals aren't tempted. In bear country, hang food off the ground, or arrange pans to clatter if food is disturbed.

Soak dried fruits overnight, they'll cook better in the morning. Make milk and let stand overnight; it improves the flavor.

Don't eat too soon after your day's hike when you're exhausted. Food digests better when you're rested. Eat attentively.

SANITATION

A proper toilet will be a hole six to eight inches deep. A shallower hole might be dug up by animals, a deeper hole would put your waste outside the layer of soil within which it can be broken down biologically. Carry a digging tool like the aluminum half-tube tent stake recommended earlier in the book. You can't do it right kicking at the ground with your boot, or using a stick. Do it right and bury it good. Tamp down earth on top. Burn used toilet paper. Locate your toilet at least 100 feet from open water and away from trail and camp. At higher elevations where it is rocky and the soil is thin, cover waste with sprinkling of soil, enough to keep off flies yet allow waste to dry out. Don't use the dry course of an intermittent stream. Don't use potential campsites and likely sleeping spots for a toilet.

TWILIGHT

After supper there is time for ambling around camp with a hot cup of tea. You watch trout feed on insects, making that quiet sound between a pop and smack as they break water. An occasional, exuberant, arching leap completely out of water. Plop. Alpenglow. Sunset. Mosquitoes quit for the day. The first star. Westering light drops behind horizon. The air turns chill.

Now it's time for that small fire. Boil water for tea. Old friend fire. Wasn't this what you came out for? To warm by a pine-wood fire out far back with nothing but stars, air, rock, trees and water around you. Big eye-watering yawn. Fix the fire so it will burn to ash overnight. Put it out if there's a wind.

SLEEP

Stumble off to bed. Take a canteen of water and a flashlight, if you have one. Turn boots and slippers upsidedown to keep out the dew. Get into bag. Cold nylon warms fast. Except in very cold temperatures, a down bag works better if you have on fewer clothes. Perhaps a light shirt to keep the cold off your shoulders. Use folded clothes for a pillow. If you're using the torso-length sleeping pad, you can make your bed more comfortable and warm by putting folded pants, wool shirt or jacket under the lower part of the bag—under your legs and feet. Adjust the bag for ventilation.

At higher elevations you'll generally fall into deep sleep at first, then wake up in the middle of the night and experience difficulty getting back to sleep. Don't worry, it's the elevation. Relax. Rest. Sense the night, watch stars—sometimes you catch an orbiting satellite. Doze off. Nights are longer outback. You will feel rested in the morning.

BREAK CAMP

You're awake before dawn and you watch it happen. Cloudless. Pure sunrise. Out of warm bag into chilly morning air. Dress. Open out bag, shake it, and set it out to air and dry. Same with poncho and pad—they will be wet on underside from condensation. Start a pot of water boiling. A pot of hot water is handy first thing in the morning. Morning ablution and morning worship, whatever its form. Breakfast. Kitchen clean-up. Fill canteen. Get everything together and pack. Clean up camp.

Carry a plastic bag just for trash and garbage. Carry out everything that won't burn to clean ash. Don't burn plastics; the fumes can be harmful to vegetation. Aluminum foil doesn't burn or disintegrate; it must be carried out.

Hopefully you did not overcook so that you're left with waste. Don't bury garbage. Park and Forest Services prohibit the digging of pits. Thinly scatter edible garbage away from camp and trail. Animals will find and eat it. Cleaning fish, never throw entrails into a stream. Bury them in a hole six to eight inches deep. Burn cans, then smash them, and pack them out.

The ideal is not to leave a trace of your stay. Double-check the fireplace. See that the fire is dead out. If the ashes are still warm, wet them down thoroughly. Rake out nonburnable items from ashes, both yours and any left by previous camp-

178

ers. Lay in some clean sand or dirt. As far as you can, make every wilderness trip a clean-up trip.

If this were a new camp and you'd made a fireplace, you would break it down, put the rocks back where they came from with the blackened side under, and scatter the dead ashes in some inconspicuous place. You would have restored the ground to its former condition.

You are packed and ready to start the day's walk. You enjoyed this camp. Stand quiet a moment and thank the place. Have you forgotten anything? You are leaving a clean camp and a dead fire. Let wilderness be protected by a ring of devotees.

OUT

You made it. You went in and you came out. You did your trip. It was both harder and easier than you thought it would be. It was harder physical exertion than you anticipated, but it was easier than you imagined keeping the trip together. The beauty of wilderness was overwhelming, both over-all and in detail. It took you far away from your usual frame of mind and gave you a long perspective on your life.

Now there are some things you won't do anymore, and there are those new things you feel but can't see the shape of yet. You understand who you are a little better. You got some work done on your secret puzzles. You pounded out a few conundrums on the trail. You got to know your friends better. Outdoor fellowship is special.

You went in fat and you came out lean. You came out with a greater respect for your body. You are going to treat it better now and stay in shape for the next time.

You saw your head through some changes. You started out nervous and excited—like a virgin. Then the hard work of backpacking got to you, and you went into a more serious mood. That broke as you acclimatized, and the trip became pure delight. Each trip has a high point. A point when you feel absolutely with it. You can't plan it. But when you get there, you know it's what you came out for.

180

Then as you neared the end of your trip, you found your head less in wilderness, even as you were in it, and more and more into thoughts of home. What's happening back there? What have you missed? You began thinking of extraordinary things you'll do once back. The foods you're going to eat—you're starving! You began to feel awfully deprived so that when you finally got back to the roadhead you felt positively liberated.

How strange, because when you finally saw the cars and people, heard the radios and mean dogs barking, you wanted to go right back into wilderness. You felt the strangeness of our civilization. How foreign it is to the part of your nature that blossomed in wilderness.

But you're out. You went away and you came back. Now as you head back to civilization, you have a wildness in your heart that wasn't there before. You know you're going outback again.

APPENDIX

RECOMMENDED READING

BACKGROUND

Evans-Wentz, W.Y. (ed.), *Tibet's Great Yogi Milarepa*, Oxford

Kroeber, Theodora, *Ishi in Two Worlds*, University of California Press

Muir, John, *Gentle Wilderness—The Sierra Nevada*, Sierra Club Books

Muir, John, *The Mountains of California*, Doubleday-Anchor

Muir, John, *The Yosemite*, Doubleday-Anchor

Snyder, Gary, *Turtle Island*, New Directions

Thompson, Stith (ed.), *Tales of the American Indians*, Indiana University Press

Thoreau, Henry David, *The Maine Woods*. All of Thoreau is worth reading. Read some of the *Journal* (Dover)—the description of his last climb onto Monadnock is very fine.

EQUIPMENT

Backpacker (ed.), *Backpacking Equipment: A Consumer Guide*

Cunningham, G.A., *How to Keep Warm*, Colorado Outdoor Sports Co. Pamphlet, available at any Gerry dealer.

Cunningham, G.A., and Hansson, M., *Lightweight Camping Equipment and How To Make It*, Colorado Outdoor Sports Co.

The *North Face* catalog is the model outdoor store catalog. A close reading of a catalog like this can teach you a great deal about equipment. Informative and up front about their stuff. *Moor and Mountain* also sends out a fine catalog. See the list of outdoor stores on pages 186-187.

FOOD

Berglund, Berndt, and Bolsby, Clare E., *The Edible Wild*, Scribners

Bunnelle, Hasse, and Thomas, Winnie, *Food for Knapsackers and Other Trail Travelers*, Sierra Club Books

Cross, Margaret, and Fisk, Jean, *Backpacker's Cookbook*, Ten Speed Press (Berkeley, CA)

Davis, Adelle, *Let's Eat Right to Keep Fit*, Harcourt

Kinmont, Vikki, and Axcell, Claudia, *Simple Foods for the Pack*, Sierra Club Books

Lappe, Frances Moore, *Diet for a Small Planet*, Ballantine

Medsger, Oliver Perry, *Edible Wild Plants*, Macmillan

Mendenhall, Ruth Dyar, *Backpack Cookery*, La Siesta Press (Glendale, CA)

Nagy, Jean, *Brown Bagging It*, Marty/Nagy Bookworks (San Francisco, CA)

TRAIL GUIDES

Moor and Mountain, Andover, MA 01810, has an excellent selection of trail guides covering both the eastern and western parts of the United States. Write for their catalog.

Sierra Club Books offers a series of Totebooks designed for a jeans pocket and covering such subjects as: *Climber's Guide to Yosemite Valley, Hiker's Guide to the Smokies, Hiking the Bigfoot Country, Hiking the Teton Backcountry, Hiking the Yellowstone Backcountry, Starr's Guide to the John Muir Trail, Climber's Guide to the High Sierra,* and more.

GENERAL

Angier, Bradford, *How to Stay Alive in the Woods,* Collier

Cunningham, G.A., *How to Camp and Leave No Trace,* Colorado Outdoor Sports Co. Pamphlet, available at any Gerry dealer.

Department of the Army, *FM 21-76 Survival, Evasion and Escape,* U.S. Government Printing Office

Fletcher, Colin, *The Complete Walker,* Knopf

Hare, F.K., *The Restless Atmosphere,* Harper and Row

Hart, John, *Walking Softly in the Wilderness,* Sierra Club Books

Kephart, Horace, *Camping and Woodcraft,* Macmillan. For its backwoods lore.

Kjellstrom, Bjorn, *Be Expert with Map and Compass,* American Orienteering Service

Lathrop, Theodore G., M.D., *Hypothermia: Killer of the Unprepared*, Mazamas

Maricopa County Department of Civil Defense and Emergency Services, *Desert Survival*

Mitchell, Dick, *Mountaineering First Aid*, The Mountaineers (Seattle, WA)

Power, John, and Brown, Jeremy, *The Fisherman's Handbook*, Scribners

Scharff, Robert, *Canada's Mountain National Parks*, McKay

Scorer, Richard, and Wexler, Harry, *A Colour Guide to Clouds*, Macmillan

Van Lear, Denise (ed.), *The Best About Backpacking*, Sierra Club Books

PERIODICALS

American Alpine Journal, The American Alpine Club, 113 E. 90th Street, New York, NY 10028

Backpacker, 65 Adams Street, Bedford Hills, NY 10507

Mountain Gazette, 2025 York Street, Denver, CO 80206

Off Belay, 15630 S.E. 124th Street, Renton, WA 98055

Summit, P.O. Box 1889, Big Bear Lake, CA 92315

Wilderness Camping, 1597 Union Street, Schenectady, NY 12309

SOME LEADING OUTDOOR CLUBS

Appalachian Trail Conference, P.O. Box 236, Harpers Ferry, West Virginia 25425

Federation of Western Outdoor Clubs, 4534½ University Way N.E., Seattle, Washington 98188

The National Audubon Society, 950 3rd Avenue, New York, New York 10028

National Hiking and Ski Touring Association, P.O. Box 7421, Colorado Springs, Colorado 80907

New York-New Jersey Trail Conference, G.P.O. Box 2250, New York, New York 10001

Sierra Club, Information Services, 530 Bush Street, San Francisco, California 94104

CANADA

Alpine Club of Canada, P.O. Box 1026, Banff, Alberta T0L 0C0

Bruce Trail Association, 33 Hardale Crescent, Hamilton, Ontario L8T 1X7

Canadian Youth Hostels Association, 333 River Road, Vanier City, Ottawa, Ontario K1L 8B9

Federation of Mountain Clubs of British Columbia, P.O. Box 33768, Station D, Vancouver 9, British Columbia V6J 4L6

Skyline Trail Hikers of the Canadian Rockies, Box 3514, Station B, Calgary, Alberta T2M 4M2

SOME OUTDOOR STORES
WITH MAIL-ORDER CATALOGS

Appalachian Outfitters, 2938 Chain Bridge Road, P.O. Box 249, Oakton, Virginia 22124

Camp and Hike Shop, 4674 Knight-Arnold Road, Memphis, Tennessee 38118

Co-op Wilderness Supply, 1607 Shattuck Avenue, Berkeley, California 94709

Eddie Bauer, P.O. Box 3700, Third & Virginia, Seattle, Washington 98124

Frostline Kits, 452 Burbank, Broomfield, Colorado 80020

Gander Mountain, Inc., P.O. Box 248, Wilmot, Wisconsin 53192

Herter's, Inc., Rural Rt. 1, Waseca, Minnesota 56093

Holubar, P.O. Box 7, Boulder, Colorado 80306

Hy-Score, 200 Tillary Street, Brooklyn, New York 11201

Kelty, 1801 Victory Boulevard, Glendale, California 91201

Laacke & Joys, 1433 N. Water Street, Milwaukee, Wisconsin 53202

L.L. Bean, Freeport, Maine 04033

Moor and Mountain, 63 Park Street, Andover, Massachusetts 01810

The North Face, P.O. Box 2399, Station A, Berkeley, California 94702

Recreational Equipment, Inc., 1525 11th Avenue, Seattle, Washington 98122

Sierra Designs, Mail Order Dept., 247 Fourth Street, Oakland, California 94607

The Ski Hut, 1615 University Avenue, Berkeley, California 94703

CANADA

Margesson's, 17 Adelaide Street E., Toronto, Ontario M5C 1H4

Thomas Black and Sons, 225 Strathcona Avenue, Ottawa, Ontario K1S 1X7

SOME METRIC EQUIVALENTS

degrees Fahrenheit (°F) – 32 X 5 ÷ 9 = degrees
    Celsius (°C)
degrees Celsius (°C) x 9 ÷ 5 + 32 = degrees Fahren-
    heit (°F)

0°F   = –18°C   250°F = 121°C
32°F   = 0°C   300°F = 149°C
70°F   = 21°C   350°F = 177°C
98.6°F = 37°C   400°F = 205°C

1 inch = 25 millimeters (mm)   1 mm = 0.04 inches
1 foot = 30 centimeters (cm)   1 cm = 0.4 inches
1 yard = 0.9 meters (m)   1 m   = 1.1 yards
1 mile = 1.6 kilometers (km)   1 km = 0.6 miles

1 ounce = 28.35 gm   1 gm = 0.032 ounce
1 pound = 0.45 kg = 454 gm   1 kg   = 2.2 pounds

1 teaspoon   = 5 milliliters (ml)
1 tablespoon = 15 ml
1 cup   = 236 ml
1 pint   = 473 ml
1 quart   = .941 liter (l)
1 gallon   = 3.785 l
1 ml   = 0.2 (1/5) teaspoon
1 ml   = 0.068 tablespoon
1 l   = 4.2 cups
1 l   = 1.057 quarts

INDEX

The brothers Saijo were born in California and have lived most of their lives there. Presently they live just north of San Francisco in what is known as North Coastal Redwood Forest with Mixed Evergreens. Coastal Fog Belt. Coastal Range where it is interrupted by San Francisco Bay. Albert is a student of natural history, and his interest in back-packing derives from wanting to be in the field for nature study. He is very close with trees and the general lay of the land. Gompers is a carpenter, artist, natural history illustrator. He is a member of the California Native Plants Society.